T3-BPE-239

THE FINANCIAL ANALYST'S DESKBOOK:

A Cash Flow Approach to Liquidity

THE FINANCIAL ANALYST'S DESKBOOK:

A Cash Flow Approach to Liquidity

JAMES W. HENDERSON
Baylor University

TERRY S. MANESS, CCM
Baylor University

Van Nostrand Reinhold / *New York*

Copyright © 1989 by Van Nostrand Reinhold.

Library of Congress Catalog Card Number
ISBN 0-442-26453-4

Printed in the United States of America.

Designed by M.R.P. Design.

Van Nostrand Reinhold
115 Fifth Avenue
New York, New York 10003

Van Nostrand Reinhold International Company Limited
11 New Fetter Lane
London EC4P 4EE, England

Van Nostrand Reinhold
480 La Trobe Street
Melbourne, Victoria 3000, Australia

Macmillan of Canada
Division of Canada Publishing Corporation
164 Commander Boulevard
Agincourt, Ontario M1S 3C7, Canada

16 15 14 13 12 11 10 9 8 7 6 5 4 3 2 1

Library of Congress Cataloging in Publication Data
Henderson, James W.
    The financial analyst's deskbook : a cash flow approach to
liquidity / James W. Henderson, Terry S. Maness.
        p.   cm.
    Includes index.
    ISBN 0-442-26453-4
    1. Cash flow.   2. Liquidity (Economics)   I. Maness, Terry S.
II. Title
HG4028.C45H46 1989
658.1'5244 — dc19

88-21731
CIP

To: Betsy, Luke, and Jesse
Nancy, Amy, and David

Contents

Preface

Financial analysis is currently undergoing a dramatic change in focus. For many years analysis of financial statements and the financial condition of firms were determined by ratios developed from the balance sheet and income statement. Then the accounting profession recognized that financial analysis could be enhanced with the generation of a third financial statement — the statement of changes in financial position. This statement showed more clearly where funds originated and where they were applied. As a result, financial analysis expanded to include the array of traditional financial ratios based on the balance sheet and income statement, along with information from the statement of changes in financial position. Since cash flow was considered a relevant financial item, it was defined as net income plus noncash charges and used in several ratios.

In 1975, W.T. Grant, a large national retailing organization, declared bankruptcy, taking the financial community by surprise. Later research showed that even though Grant's operations showed a profit up to the year it declared bankruptcy, by using a more precise definition of cash flow, its operation was a net user of cash for eight out of ten years before bankruptcy. This event more than anything else pointed out the limitations of accrual-based ratios and their focus on profitability as a measure of operating performance. It also emphasized the need for a clearer focus on liquidity and financial flexibility, that is, the cash flow approach.

Now everyone is voicing the praises of cash flow analysis. Lenders are analyzing cash flow before making loans; corporate raiders are intent on estimating free cash flow in evaluating takeover candidates. The problems have been that until recently there was no standard definition of cash flow and there were no standard ratios that included an accurate measure of cash flow as a part of the ratio.

The accounting profession has taken an important step forward in standardizing cash flow definitions through the *Statement of Financial Accounting Standards No. 95* (FASB 95). This new accounting standard requires a statement of cash flow to replace the statement of changes in financial position. The statement provides definitions for three different measures of cash flow—cash flow from operations, cash flow from investing activities, and cash flow from financing activities.

This book provides an organized approach to assessing the liquidity position of a firm through the analysis of cash flow. It discusses a wide array of liquidity measures that have emerged over the last several years as well as develops some new measures. In addition, it establishes an organizational framework for liquidity analysis.

Chapter 1 provides background and important definitions. **Chapter 2** discusses traditional financial statement analysis using standard accrual-based ratios. **Chapter 3** develops the new statement of cash flow consistent with FASB 95. Chapters 4 to 8 develop tools and techniques for analyzing liquidity and financial flexibility based on the cash flow statement.

Chapter 4 focuses on the analysis of cash flow from operations. **Chapter 5** broadens the focus by including in the analysis cash flow from investing activities and cash flow from financing activities. Together they organize currently existing liquidity measures as well as develop new measures of liquidity and financial flexibility.

Chapter 6 presents four case studies using the measures discussed and developed in Chapters 4 and 5. W. T. Grant is analyzed as the classic case of a profitable yet cash poor company. Chrysler Corporation is studied for its value as a major corporate turnaround. John Deere and Company is viewed as an operation in transition. Phillips Petroleum Company is studied as a firm in the process of subverting a takeover attempt. **Chapter 7** presents special topics, including cash flow and bankruptcy analysis, the impact of inflation on liquidity, assessing the quality of earnings, and liquidity and the small business.

Chapter 8 discusses the use of the microcomputer as a tool to conduct financial analysis. It presents a primer on electronic spreadsheets focusing on Lotus 1-2-3™ and develops a template for the new statement of cash flow giving cell references. The book concludes with a glossary.

Acknowledgments

In writing this book, we received helpful comments from many people. We would especially like to thank our colleagues Tom Harrison and John T. Rose for their special insights, and Susan Riffe, who was invaluable in helping us with the literature research.

THE FINANCIAL
ANALYST'S
DESKBOOK:

A Cash Flow
Approach to
Liquidity

Chapter 1

Defining Cash Flow

Users of financial statements have traditionally relied on ratio analysis as a major tool in evaluating the financial strength of a business enterprise. Financial ratios, derived from accrual-based financial statements, are used primarily to measure one aspect of operating performance — namely, profitability. Although profitability analysis is an important aspect of a complete financial evaluation, it is by no means the only one and may not even be the most important.

The most significant aspect of financial health not adequately measured by financial ratios is *liquidity*. Accrual-based liquidity ratios, for example, current and quick ratios, are available for this purpose. There are, however, two basic problems with these measures: (1) They use a working capital definition of funds in measuring liquidity, and (2) they view liquidity from a solvency or liquidation perspective.

In contrast, the appropriate definition of funds for measuring liquidity considers the timing of cash inflows and outflows; that is, how long it takes to convert an asset into cash and how long until a liability comes due. In addition, the proper perspective for liquidity analysis is that of a going concern, not a liquidated operation. Operating managers do not consider strategies that require converting all receivables and inventories into cash and paying off all short-term obligations. But rather, they are interested in the short-term ability of the operation to meet immediate cash needs and the long-term ability to generate cash from external sources.

Campbell, Johnson, and Savoie (1984) surveyed corporate treasurers on the importance of twenty-one factors in their firm's liquidity management and planning. Results of the survey show that the respondents placed more emphasis on cash flow analysis than on traditional ratio analysis in monitoring liquidity. Short-term cash flow projections were ranked as the most important tool for tracking corporate liquidity. Monitoring accounts receivable and inventory was also considered extremely important. Surprisingly, the use of traditional ratio analysis ranked eighteenth in importance out of the twenty-one possible responses.

The results of this survey suggest that individuals responsible for monitoring liquidity should reconsider the traditional emphasis on ratio analysis. Other measures of liquidity and financial flexibility may provide managers with better information on a firm's ability to generate cash. Cash flow projections, inventory and receivables management, aggregate lines of credit, and sound banking relationships are relied on most heavily for this purpose.

Accrual-basis accounting continues to provide valuable information on the operating performance of a firm. Traditional ratio analysis, based on financial statements prepared on accrual-based concepts, provides valid information on the financial health and performance of a business operation. Ratios are fundamental indicators of business profitability and should be used as a starting point in the financial analysis. In other words, whenever profitability is the issue, accrual-based statements provide invaluable information.

If, however, the goal is to study liquidity and financial flexibility, the use of accrual-based concepts can be misleading, since revenues and expenses may not match cash receipts and disbursements. Accrual-based financial statements are prepared to reflect profitability by adhering to the fundamental accounting precept referred to as the *matching principle*. Under the matching principle, only revenues and expenses that apply to current-period transactions are included in the calculation of profit or loss, regardless of the associated cash inflows and outflows.

Fortunately, it is possible to restructure the accrual-based financial statements to analyze liquidity and financial flexibility. The traditional statement of changes in financial position using a cash definition of funds can be presented in a meaningful format to facilitate cash flow analysis and planning. The format restructures the balance sheet and income statement accounts to reverse the effects of accrual-basis accounting and show how funds have flowed into and out of the operation.

Interpreting what the accrual and cash flow indicators are saying about an operation is fairly straightforward when the two are in agreement. There is little doubt about the financial health of an unprofitable operation with a negative cash flow or a profitable one with a positive cash flow. It is the profitable company with a negative cash flow or the unprofitable company with a positive cash flow that presents a more complex analytical problem. A profitable company with an expanding asset base or shrinking liabilities will often show negative cash flow. In contrast, an unprofitable company with a shrinking asset base or expanding liabilities can show positive cash flow. In both cases, it is essential to understand the causes and implications of the behavior in order to interpret the accrual and cash indicators correctly.

Combining the two approaches will prove useful in providing insights and identifying potential problem areas. The first step toward this objective is to define cash flow and carefully outline the cash flow approach to analyzing liquidity and financial flexibility.

CASH FLOW APPROACH

Cash flow and its interpretation have gained considerable attention in the financial accounting literature in recent years. Historically, the task of developing a complete conceptual framework for financial reporting has been placed in the hands of the Financial Accounting Standards Board (FASB). The FASB has been very active in reporting on various aspects of the cash flow issue.

Historical Developments

In 1971, the Accounting Principles Board (APB) Opinion No. 19 was issued requiring that a statement of changes in financial position (SCFP) be included in a set of financial statements and that it be covered by the auditor's opinion. It was the view of the Board

> that information concerning the financing and investing activities of a business enterprise and the changes in its financial position for a period is essential for financial statement users, particularly owners and creditors, in making economic decisions. When financial statements . . . are issued, a statement summarizing changes in financial position should also be presented as a basic financial statement. . . . These conclusions apply to all profit-oriented business entities. (AICPA, 1971)

Although the Board required the inclusion of the SCFP, it continued to allow considerable flexibility in the manner in which it was presented. A company, for example, was allowed to prepare the statement using various definitions of funds: cash, cash plus cash equivalents, or working capital.

Over the next decade, it became evident that although the reporting flexibility was good in some respects, it led to a great deal of confusion for those who tried to compare operating results across companies. In a 1981 exposure draft, *Reporting Income, Cash Flows and Financial Position of a Business Enterprise*, the FASB suggested that a cash definition of funds was the most useful. By this time the SCFP had become an integral part of the financial reporting of a firm and an essential ingredient in a complete financial analysis. Thus, comparability across firms was slowly being recognized as important.

Concepts Statement No. 1, *Objectives of Financial Reporting by Business Enterprises* (1983), took the issue one step farther. It indicated that "financial reporting should provide information to help investors, creditors, and others assess the amounts, timing, and uncertainty of prospective net cash inflows." Although this statement did not require that cash flow information be included in financial reporting, it did recognize that "information about cash flows or other funds flows may be useful in understanding the operations of an enterprise, evaluating its financing activities, assessing its liquidity or solvency, or interpreting earnings information provided" (FASB, 1983, pp. 17, 21).

In Concepts Statement No. 5 (1985), the FASB recognized the importance of the cash flow statement and concluded that conceptually "the cash flow statement should be part of a full set of financial statements." By 1985 the Board seriously began to consider requiring the cash flow statement in place of the SCFP. Before the cash flow statement was to become mandatory, however, it was determined that objectives for the statement should first be established and certain major cash flow concepts be defined.

In November 1987, the task had been completed and the Board issued its *Statement of Financial Accounting Standards No. 95*, Statement of Cash Flows (Financial Accounting Series, 1987) requiring the cash flow statement in place of the statement of changes in financial position for all fiscal periods ending after July 15, 1988. The restatement of financial statements for earlier years is encouraged but not required. The proposal also established objectives for the cash flow statement and definitions of key cash concepts. Although this policy was significant, it may be viewed simply as a reaction to current industry practices. *Accounting Trends and Techniques* (Shohet and Rikert, 1982) reports that fully two-thirds of the financial statements generated by publicly held corporations in the United States at that time already used cash instead of working capital for purposes of the statement of changes in financial position.

Defining Cash Flow

The simplest way to conceptualize cash flow is to think of it as a process wherein cash flows into and out of a business operation. In summarizing current cash receipts and disbursements, the cash flow statement provides information not only on liquidity, but also on financial flexibility, profitability, and risk. With the passage of FASB 95, the importance of the cash flow statement is no longer an issue. The major concern is understanding the concept of cash flow.

The basic problem in developing a cash-basis analytical framework is that most users of financial statements do not have a clear understanding of cash flow or a knowledge of how it is calculated. Even more importantly, very few have the ability to interpret cash flow and cash flow trends in relation to company objectives and industry norms.

The objective of cash flow analysis is to evaluate how effective an operation has been in generating cash internally to support its incremental asset requirements caused by sales growth and cover the costs of financing, including interest expense on term debt and the payment of dividends. With this objective in mind, *cash flow from operations* (CFFO) is defined in Table 1-1 as cash receipts from sales minus cash expenditures related to sales.

Cash receipts from sales is defined as current period net sales plus cash collections from prior period sales minus current period sales uncollected (i.e., the change in accounts receivable). Cash disbursements related to sales is defined as cash expenditures for production costs (cost of sales adjusted for changes in inventory plus cash payments for prior period inventory purchases minus current period purchases unpaid), operating expenses (not including depreciation expense and adjusted for changes in prepaids), and taxes (adjusted for changes in accruals and deferred taxes). Only if a concern is generating a positive cash flow using this definition does it have the cash available from internal (spontaneous) sources to expand its asset base and cover

TABLE 1-1.   The Component Parts of Cash Flow from Operations

+*Cash receipts from sales*

    Net Sales
    −Change in accounts receivable
    =Cash receipts from sales

−*Cash expenditures related to sales*

    Cost of sales
    +Change in inventory
    −Change in accounts payable
    +Operating expenses (excluding depreciation)
    +Change in prepaids and accruals
    +Taxes
    −Change in accrued and deferred taxes
    =Cash expenditures related to sales

=*Cash flow from operations*

financing costs, including the repayment of principal on loans and dividends to shareholders.

Using the distinctions outlined in FASB 95, cash is defined as including cash and cash equivalents. *Cash equivalents* are defined as short-term, highly-liquid investments that are readily converted into known amounts of cash or are so close to maturity that the risk of changes in value due to changes in interest rates is insignificant. Generally, only investments with original maturities of less than 3 months qualify.

This definition takes into consideration the common practice of investing excess cash in highly liquid, short-term instruments such as treasury bills, certificates of deposit, money market funds, and commercial paper. This practice is formally considered part of the cash management activity of the firm, not an investing activity; thus, details of these transactions do not have to be reported. When assessing the cash flow of an operation, it is of minor consequence if the cash is on hand, on deposit, or invested in highly liquid, short-term instruments. The distinction is not significant enough to warrant separate treatment.

Relationship between Working Capital and Cash Flow

Historically, *working capital* served as the funds concept for the majority of the firms required to publish financial data. The popularity of this approach was based on a notion that equated liquidity with solvency. The direct result of this misconception is that most financial analysts active today were taught that working capital is the best measure of a firm's ability to meet its financial obligations. This is still a popular view held by many in the financial community.

Working capital from operations is a widely disclosed figure on many pre-1988 financial statements regardless of format. Because of this and the familiarity with the working capital concept, it is beneficial to show the connection that exists among the concepts of net income, working capital from operations, and cash flow from operations.

In simple terms, *working capital from operations* (WCFO) is an adjustment of net income for long-term accruals, deferrals, and other allocations that produce revenues and expenses but do not affect current balance sheet accounts. Since these adjustments do not affect the flow of funds, they must either be added to or subtracted from net income to counteract their original impact. The calculation is summarized in Table 1-2, Part A.

Cash flow from operations can be calculated by adjusting working capital from operations by the short-term accruals, deferrals, and other allocations that do not represent sources and uses of cash. The calculation is shown in Table 1-2, Part B.

TABLE 1-2. Calculating Working Capital from Operations and Cash Flow from Operations from Net Income

Part A: Working Capital from Operations Equals

Net income
Adjustments for items not requiring working capital
  Plus depreciation, depletion, and amortization
  Plus (minus) increase (decrease) in deferred income taxes payable and deferred tax credits
  Plus (minus) undistributed equity method[a] losses (income)
  Plus (minus) amortization of discount (premium) on bonds payable
  Plus (minus) amortization of premium (discount) on bond investment
  Plus (minus) losses (gains) on nonoperating items

Part B: Cash Flow from Operations Equals

Working capital from operations
Adjustments for items not affecting cash
  Plus (minus) decrease (increase) in accounts and notes receivable due to trade
  Plus (minus) decrease (increase) in inventories
  Plus (minus) decrease (increase) in prepaids
  Plus (minus) increase (decrease) in accounts payable and notes payable due to trade
  Plus (minus) increase (decrease) in accruals

[a]Losses or income in excess of cash dividends recognized from unconsolidated stock investments.

Although net income, working capital from operations, and cash flow from operations are all important indicators of the financial health of a firm, it is incorrect to assume that similar conclusions can be reached about liquidity, financial flexibility, and risk using any measure of cash flow (Gombola and Ketz, 1981). The most commonly used indicators of liquidity are net income plus depreciation, cash flow from operations, and working capital from operations. They cannot be used interchangeably except under very restrictive assumptions. Only if the following two conditions are met can net income plus depreciation or working capital from operations be substituted for cash flow from operations. First, depreciation expense must be the only significant expense that does not affect net working capital. Second, net working capital items, such as accounts receivable, inventory, and accounts payable, must not change significantly or their changes must offset one another.

Cash flow from operations is a distinctive measure of the cash consequences of profit-directed activities of a firm and is not systematically correlated with any other performance measure commonly used. Only CFFO adequately separates the operating activities of the firm from the investing and financing activities. It is ultimately CFFO that determines whether an entity is capable of generating cash to repay debt, distribute dividends, or reinvest in plant and equipment to maintain or expand operations.

MANAGING CASH FLOW

The actual process of managing cash flow is more than a matter of defining cash flow and preparing cash flow statements; it is one of managing the timing of receipts and expenditures. In the long run, cash inflows and cash outflows must at least be in balance for the firm to survive. That is not to say that an occasional period of negative cash flow is not to be tolerated under any circumstances. The phenomenon may be caused by seasonal factors outside the control of management or it may even be encouraged if, for example, inventories can be purchased in bulk amounts at a considerable savings to the firm.

Cash flow management requires an understanding of the relationships involved and a systematic means of planning and control. The key to such a mechanism is the availability of information and the ability to process and use that information. An important feature of a cash management system is an accounting system that will provide the necessary information to anticipate and plan for the timing of cash inflows and outflows.

The goal of a cash management system is to minimize the nonproductive use of cash balances. This is not as simple as it may seem. It requires much more than keeping idle cash balances at a minimum and delaying cash disbursements. It involves the effective use of techniques that shorten each aspect of the cash flow cycle. In other words, successful cash management involves effective management of accounts payable, accounts receivable, and inventories.

The most important planning tool in the cash management system is a reliable cash flow forecast. Often referred to as a *cash budget*, it is beneficial in two important ways. First, it reduces uncertainty and thus leads to a reduced demand for precautionary cash balances. Second, it provides for advanced warning of impending cash flow deficits and gives management more time to respond with carefully constructed solutions.

A cash flow forecast is simply a report that represents the cash flow cycle. To prepare a cash budget, the first step is to analyze the cash flow statement prepared from historical data. This information serves as a basis for preparing the cash budget that relates to the future operation of the firm. The key to successful cash flow forecasts is more a matter of understanding the concepts and relationships in the cash flow cycle than it is making additional reports and calculations.

CASH FLOW CYCLE

A positive cash flow is essential to the long-term viability of any business operation. What may seem like a trivial observation is critically important, particularly for the startup and high-growth business venture. Cash flow is the lifeblood of a business operation. In much the same way that a living organism functions improperly without an adequate blood supply, a business will suffer without an adequate cash flow.

Simple Cash Flow Cycle

A thorough understanding of the *cash flow cycle* is essential in order to initiate a cash planning and cash control system within an operation. A simple cash flow cycle is illustrated in Figure 1-1. For the sake of brevity and clarity, the focus of this section is solely on the short-term cycle. Each box depicts a stock account. The flows leading into and out of the boxes show the productive activities that sustain the operation.

In Figure 1-1, the cash cycle begins when cash is used to initiate the production process (i.e., to purchase inventories). As customers demand the product, inventories are sold, thereby generating profits in the accrual sense but not necessarily cash. Whether or not a sale completes the cash cycle (resulting in an increase in the cash account) depends on whether it is a cash or a credit sale. Cash sales flow directly into the cash account; credit sales flow into an accounts receivable account. Credit sales do not complete the cash cycle until accounts receivable are collected.

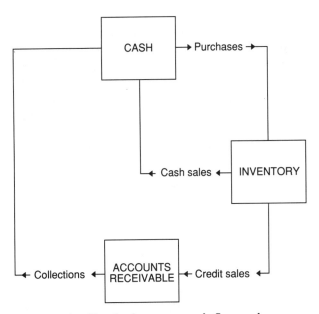

Figure 1-1. Simple short-term cash flow cycle.

Given the nature of the cash flow cycle, the functioning of the system depends on the relative rates of the flows into and out of each account. If purchases exceed sales, the inventory account increases and the accounts receivable and cash accounts decrease. A slowdown in credit collections will result in a buildup in the receivables account and a reduction in the cash account, illustrating that a change in one area of the system has repercussions in all the other areas of the operation.

Complete Cash Flow Cycle

The complete cash flow cycle incorporates the various aspects of long-term decision making into the system. This includes decisions regarding fixed assets and external funding sources — long-term debt and ownership equity.

Figure 1-2 presents the complete cash flow cycle. In addition to the stock accounts in Figure 1-1, there are three others that represent long-term decisions — fixed assets, creditors' funds, and owners' funds — and two that are included to distinguish between cash and credit purchases — the accounts payable account and the suppliers' funds account. The productive activities associated with these stock accounts are also indicated in the figure.

Cash purchases flow directly into the inventory account as shown in Figure 1-1. The addition of the accounts payable and suppliers' funds accounts results in a separate outflow representing the repayment of accounts payable and a noncash activity depicting the extension of trade credit represented by an inflow from suppliers' funds. The trade credit inflow is countered by a credit purchases outflow into the inventory account. Most operations will incur various expenses in connection with making the product ready for the market. This activity is shown by a cash outflow representing operating expenses (excluding depreciation expense) from the cash account into the inventory account. If depreciation expense were included in the figure as a separate activity, it would be shown as a flow from the fixed asset account to the inventory account.

Expanding the figure to take into consideration the long-term investing and financing activities of the firm will provide the complete cash cycle. The purchase and sale of fixed assets are, respectively, the cash outflow and cash inflow representing the investment activities of the firm.

External financing of some type is required to initiate the operation and ensure that it is able to satisfy market demand for its product. The addition of separate accounts depicting creditors' funds and owners' funds represent the financing activities of the firm. In Figure 1-2, the respective cash inflows from these two accounts are shown as borrowings

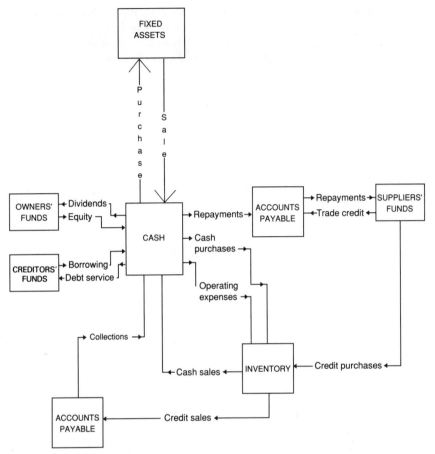

Figure 1-2. Complete cash flow cycle.

and equity; cash outflows are shown as debt service and dividends (or owners' draw if a proprietorship or partnership).

The principles of managing the cash flow system in Figure 1-2 are identical to those of managing the simple system in Figure 1-1. The addition of activities merely complicates the task of keeping the stock accounts at their optimal levels and the rate of the inflows and outflows balanced.

Not all cash outflows have been considered in Figure 1-2. Many leakages from the system may also be incorporated into the analysis, including inventory losses, bad debt losses, losses from the sale of assets, and taxes. Although these leakages are ignored, they do exist and play a significant role in the complete cash flow planning model.

To reflect the cash flow process for a manufacturing operation accurately, the cash flow cycle in Figure 1-2 would need to be refined and expanded. Instead of just considering inventories, it would be necessary to include raw materials, work-in-process, and finished goods inventories. To read about these details, see Kreps and Wacht (1978).

FINANCING GAP

The source of most cash flow problems experienced by a typical firm is in the area of accounts receivable and inventory turnover. Most firms pay suppliers for inventories before the goods are sold to customers. Also, if credit is granted to purchasers, there is an additional lag between when goods are sold and when payment is received.

A low rate of inventory turnover can be an acute problem, but a high rate also tends to present problems that are critical. This phenomenon, referred to as *overtrading,* is a characteristic of an undercapitalized operation. A relatively small inventory can easily result in the inability to meet customer demand for certain items. The result is lost sales and a reduced cash flow, which makes the firm vulnerable to a slowdown in the collections of accounts receivable.

Rapid growth often results in a significant buildup of receivables and inventory, even if turnover rates are constant. When this absorption of cash is not offset spontaneously by increases in payables and accruals, the result is a *financing gap.* The financing gap is the reason firms can be profitable and illiquid at the same time.

The implications of these phenomena are far reaching. Of primary importance to the emerging firm is the impact on its ability to sustain even a modest rate of sales growth. It is because of the financing gap that sales growth often exceeds the firm's ability to finance that growth through internally generated funds. Liquidity becomes a problem as a firm's dependency on external financing increases substantially. The less liquid a firm, the greater its reliance on external (nonspontaneous) financing sources. For the firm experiencing liquidity problems, sales growth can be a problem if its financial position is highly leveraged or credit lines are unavailable.

SUMMARY

Cash flow analysis should be used in conjunction with traditional ratio analysis to get a complete picture of the financial position of a firm. Cash flow analysis focuses on liquidity, and accrual-based ratio analysis focuses on profitability. Each approach, when used in isolation from the other, ignores an important aspect of financial health. In today's rapidly changing business and financial environment, it is becoming increasingly important to have a complete picture of a company's financial health and performance. To that end, it is important to develop an integrated analysis of the financial condition of an ongoing operation.

REFERENCES

AICPA. Opinion of the Accounting Principles Board No. 19, 1971. *Reporting Changes in Financial Position*. New York: AICPA.

Campbell, David R., James M. Johnson, and Leonard M. Savoie. 1984. Cash Flow, Liquidity, and Financial Flexibility. *Financial Executive* 52(8):14–17.

Concepts Statement No. 1. 1983. *Objectives of Financial Reporting by Business Enterprises*. Stamford, CT: Financial Accounting Standards Board.

Concepts Statement No. 5, 1985. *Recognition and Measurement in Financial Statements of Business Enterprises*. Stamford, CT: Financial Accounting Standards Board.

Exposure Draft. November 1981. *Reporting Income, Cash Flows, and Financial Position of a Business Enterprise*. Stamford, CT: Financial Accounting Standards Board.

Financial Accounting Series. November 1987. Statement of Cash Flows. *Statement of Financial Accounting Standards No. 95*. Stamford, CT: Financial Accounting Standards Board.

Gombola, Michael J., and J. Edward Ketz. 1983. A Note on Cash Flow and Classification Patterns of Financial Ratios. *The Accounting Review* 58(1):105–114.

———. 1981. Alternative Measures of Cash Flow: Part I. *Cashflow* 2(8):33–37.

Kreps, Clifton H., Jr., and Richard F. Wacht. 1978. *Analyzing Financial Statements*, 5th edition. Washington, DC: American Bankers Association.

Shohet, Jack, and Richard Rikert, Eds. 1982. *Accounting Trends, and Techniques*, 36th edition, New York: AICPA.

Chapter 2

Financial Accounting and Analysis

To complete a thorough financial analysis successfully, several key accounting concepts must be understood, including the difference between cash- and accrual-basis accounting, the value of a complete set of financial statements, and the technique of ratio calculation and analysis.

CASH- AND ACCRUAL-BASIS ACCOUNTING

According to *cash-basis accounting*, income is recorded when cash is actually received and expenditures are recorded when payments are actually made. This procedure is commonly used by individuals to keep track of personal income and expenditures and for certain types of businesses. When using this format, certain items do not show up on the operation's financial statements, most notably, accounts receivable, prepaid expenses, accounts payable, and accruals.

For most businesses, *accrual-basis accounting* is the preferred method of keeping track of transactions that affect property and rights to property. *Generally accepted accounting principles* (GAAP) recognize this method as the one that most accurately reflects a firm's profitability. Under accrual-basis accounting, revenues are recorded in the time period that coincides most closely to the completion of the actual transaction, regardless of when the cash payment is received. In other words, at the time a product is sold or a service rendered, there will be a bookkeeping entry showing an increase in cash (if the customer pays cash) or in accounts receivable (if the customer receives trade credit). This practice is often referred to as the *realization principle.*

Costs are incurred in the process of generating revenues. Therefore, they are recorded as expenses in the same time period the matching revenue is recorded. The purpose of the matching principle is to measure the profitability of sales during the time period by matching them with the appropriate expenses used to generate those sales.

Prepaid expenses are not treated as an expense until they are actually incurred in providing a product or service for sale. For example, an insurance premium may be paid annually; however, the pro rata share is recorded as an expense each month. This method of accounting does not consider a prepaid item an expense until it is actually used in the production process.

The goal of accrual accounting is to record revenues, expenses, gains, and losses during the time periods in which they affect company performance. As a result, performance is measured by profits and has no direct connection with the ability of a firm to generate cash flow. Current cash inflows may actually result from business activity of earlier periods, and current cash outflows may actually relate to expected future activity. The primary difference between accrual and cash accounting, therefore, is in the realization and matching principles that affect the way that revenues, expenses, gains, and losses are recorded.

BASIC FINANCIAL STATEMENTS

The results of the operation of a business enterprise are reflected in its basic financial statements: the statement of operations or income statement, the balance sheet, and the statement of changes in financial position or the cash flow statement. Collectively, they provide a summary of the firm's operations over the time periods under review and the firm's financial position at the end of each of those periods.

In addition to the quantitative information provided in the financial statements, most firms will also provide qualitative information in the form of footnotes and disclosures. The statements provide details on what has happened during the accounting period, and the footnotes provide important details that are too cumbersome to include in the body of the statements. For example, the footnotes may provide detailed schedules of notes payable and long-term debt, explanations of subsidiary investments, and information on leases, guarantees, commitments, and other contingent liabilities.

Income Statement

The 1985 and 1986 income statement for John Deere and Company is shown in Table 2-1. There are three major components: operating revenues, expenses, and profit.

TABLE 2-1. Deere's Income Statement (in thousands)

	Years Ending	
	October 1985	October 1986
Sales	$4,060,648	$3,516,289
Cost of sales	3,355,318	3,237,018
Gross profit	$ 705,330	$ 279,271
Operating expenses (excluding depreciation)	$ 535,953	$ 564,026
Depreciation and amortization	194,528	202,577
Other operating expense (income)	(95,243)	(98,408)
Total operating expenses	$ 635,238	668,195
Operating profit	$ 70,092	$ (388,924)
Interest expense	$ 199,320	$ 203,769
Nonoperating expense (income)	(95,235)	(79,485)
Before-tax profit	$ (33,993)	$ (513,207)
Income taxes (credits)	$ (64,498)	$ (283,936)
After-tax profit	$ 30,505	$ (229,272)
Dividends	$ 67,820	$ 50,881

Operating Revenues. *Operating revenues* represent actual or expected cash inflows from the sale and delivery of goods and services during an accounting period (in this case annually). To be recorded as an operating revenue, the transaction must be the result of an activity that is central to the ongoing operation, such as goods delivered or services rendered.

Operating revenues can be called sales as shown in Table 2-1, royalties, or rents depending on the specific kind of business operation. The main point is that only revenues generated as part of the major operation are recorded as operating revenues. Interest earned on a certificate of deposit, proceeds from the sale of a fixed asset, or an insurance settlement, for example, would be recorded as nonoperating or extraordinary revenues.

Expenses. Expenses represent actual or expected cash outflows that result from the sale or delivery of goods and services during an accounting period. Recorded as either cost of goods sold or operating expenses, they must result from an activity that is central to the ongoing operation.

Expenses are referred to as wages, salaries, depreciation, or advertising, depending on the specific type of business operation. Nonoperating expenses such as a major casualty loss and other items that result in the reduction of assets are listed in a separate section of the income statement.

Profit. Profit represents the difference between the revenues generated by the business operation and the corresponding expenses incurred. Various measures of profit should be highlighted, including gross profit, operating profit, before-tax profit, and after-tax profit.

Gross profit is a measure of how successful an operation is in turning merchandise inventories into profit. It is determined by the average markup on goods and services sold. A firm with an average markup of 67 percent on its merchandise, for example, has a gross profit margin of 40 percent.

Operating profit is the difference between operating revenues and operating expenses. It examines the profitability of the business attributable solely to the activities that are central to the ongoing operation. Operating profit does not take into consideration interest expense (which is determined by the way the firm is capitalized) or income taxes (which are determined by things such as organizational form and the peculiarities of the federal income tax codes).

Although before-tax profit and after-tax profit are the two most widely used measures for determining the relative performance of an operation, neither represents the addition to cash balances when the accounting records are kept on an accrual basis.

Balance Sheet

The primary purpose of the balance sheet is to show the financial position of a business operation at a particular point in time. The balance sheets for Deere for 1984 through 1986 are given in Table 2-2. The statements show the firm's financial position as of October 31, the last day of each of those fiscal years. This point becomes important when two balance sheets are viewed with their related income statements. For example, the 1984 balance sheet gives a picture of the operation at the beginning of 1985, the 1985 income statement gives a summary of the operation during that year, and the 1985 balance sheet shows the impact of the year's operation on the firm's financial position.

The balance sheet is divided into the three main components as described by the fundamental accounting identity: assets, liabilities, and capital. Each of these major categories is broken down into subcategories. Assets are listed according to the ease of converting them into cash: current assets, fixed assets, intangibles (if applicable), and other assets. Liabilities are listed in the order in which the obligations come due: current liabilities, long-term liabilities, and other liabilities. The capital account, or owners' equity account, represent owners' claims against assets and are obligations that never come due.

The owners' equity account is divided into two major areas: owners'

TABLE 2-2. Deere Balance Sheets as of October 31 (in thousands)

	1984	1985	1986
Assets			
Cash and equivalents	$ 41,323	$ 87,823	$ 181,657
Accounts receivable	3,089,042	2,894,139	2,290,254
Inventory	539,897	447,370	482,630
All other current assets	4,232	5,266	6,699
Total Current Assets	$3,674,494	$3,434,598	$2,961,240
Gross fixed assets	$2,484,074	$2,629,193	$2,767,109
Accumulated depreciation	(1,451,468)	(1,613,331)	(1,816,053)
All other noncurrent assets	990,196	1,011,767	1,061,971
Total Assets	$5,697,296	$5,462,227	$4,974,267
Liabilities and Capital			
Accounts payable	$1,125,807	$1,026,945	$ 994,459
Short-term notes payable	567,783	520,570	383,454
Accrued dividends	16,952	16,948	8,484
Accrued taxes	350,322	332,896	110,942
Current maturities long-term debt	157,833	16,351	12,078
Total Current Liabilities	$2,218,697	$1,913,710	$1,509,417
Long-term debt	$ 972,185	$1,110,087	$1,279,506
Deferred income tax	108,073	50,524	12,981
All other noncurrent liabilities	107,513	129,290	173,086
Total Liabilities	$3,406,468	$3,203,611	$2,974,990
Common stock	$ 67,991	$ 68,030	$ 68,050
Paid-in capital and other	311,038	316,158	336,957
Treasury stock	(2,725)	(2,725)	(2,725)
Retained earnings	1,914,524	1,877,153	1,596,995
Liabilities and Capital	$5,697,296	$5,462,227	$4,974,267

investment and retained earnings. The owners' investment is comprised of preferred stock, common stock, paid-in capital, and treasury stock. Both preferred and common stock represent ownership in the firm. The main distinction is that owners of preferred stock receive a fixed dividend, and owners of preferred stock have a preferential position to those of common stock in the event of a business liquidation. Paid-in capital represents the owners' investment in the business in excess of the par value of the stock purchased.

Treasury stock is common stock that has been repurchased by the company; in effect, it is negative equity. Its purchase has a significant impact on the firm's financial position. By reducing shareholders' equity, the purchase of treasury stock increases the risk to creditors in the event of a business downturn. For the investor, fewer outstanding shares can be immediately translated into higher earnings per share. If the firm's future growth potential is impaired, however, treasury stock will eventually have the opposite effect. In either case, the purchase of treasury stock results in a lowering of a firm's liquidity and leverage positions, which has a negative implication for overall financial strength.

Retained earnings is that portion of the net earnings of the firm that has been reinvested in the operation from its inception. It represents the residual equity of the operation, that portion of the owners' claims against property that has not been distributed directly through dividends. The total owners' equity is then calculated by subtracting treasury stock from the sum of preferred stock, common stock, paid-in capital, and retained earnings.

Another aspect of the balance sheet is the reconciliation of the owners' equity account. Referred to as the statement of retained earnings or the reconciliation of net worth, it can either be presented in the capital account of the balance sheet or in a separate statement.

A statement of retained earnings is based on the relationship between retained earnings shown on one year's balance sheet with that of the previous year. Presented as a formula, it can be seen that

$$
\begin{aligned}
&\text{Retained Earnings in Year 0}\\
+\ &\text{After-Tax Profit in Year 1}\\
-\ &\underline{\text{Dividends Paid in Year 1}}\\
=\ &\text{Retained Earnings in Year 1}
\end{aligned}
$$

Unless there has been a prior period adjustment to retained earnings due to changes in asset valuation, transactions in the firm's stock for other than par value, or accounting errors, this relationship should hold true. Using data from Deere, the relationship is as follows:

1984 Retained Earnings (Table 2-2)	$1,914,524
1985 After-Tax Profit (Table 2-1)	30,505
	$1,945,029
1985 Dividends Paid (Table 2-3)	67,876
1985 Retained Earnings (Table 2-2)	$1,877,153

Statement of Changes in Financial Position

The statement of changes in financial position, or funds flow statement, has been a required part of a complete set of financial statements since the early 1970s. Even though no new information is presented beyond what is already shown on the income statement and the balance sheets, the format itself provides a uniquely different perspective of the firm's financial position.

The problem with the past practice of preparing the SCFP stems from the wide latitude that preparers had been given on how concepts were to be defined or how data were to be presented. Without a clear statement of objectives, accountants were defining concepts and devising formats to suit individual objectives with no concern for comparability across entities.

Over the past decade, the lack of uniformity in the preparation of the SCFP may have been counterproductive. With accountants using different definitions of key concepts, including funds, cash, and cash flow from operations, as well as a wide variety of formats, the usefulness of the statement has been diminished. Individuals wanting to evaluate the liquidity or financial flexibility of an operation have had a difficult time monitoring changes across time or comparing them across companies.

Traditionally, accountants have used the working capital concept to define funds. Using this approach, any transaction that leads to a change in either current assets or current liabilities is shown on the SCFP. This can be misleading, since increases in working capital do not necessarily indicate increases in liquidity nor do decreases in working capital indicate decreases in liquidity. Many routine transactions, such as cash collections on accounts receivable and inventory purchased on trade credit, simply do not show up as changes in working capital. Additionally, increases in working capital may result from transactions that actually reduce liquidity rather than enhance it. Increases in working capital due to increases in inventory or accounts receivable actually use cash rather than generate it and thus fall into this category.

In this regard, the use of a cash basis to report the changes that occur in financial position is superior to the working capital approach. Any transaction that either increases or decreases cash is considered in preparing the statement. Even this approach has its limitations, because many transactions that do not result in a change in cash balances nevertheless affect an entity's financial position. For example, the funding of a purchase of fixed assets with long-term debt or equity does not affect working capital or cash. Without question, such transactions affect the financial position of a firm.

To avoid these pitfalls, the concept of changes in financial position is defined to include any change that affects the financing and investing activities of an entity. Thus, to satisfy this all-financial-resources concept, a firm must disclose all transactions that significantly affect its financial position that would otherwise be omitted, regardless of its effect on cash or working capital.

The following discussion uses the traditional approach in generating the statement of changes. Two significant characteristics mark this approach: (1) A working capital definition of funds is used, and (2) the format divides funds flow into two categories, sources and uses. The primary sources and uses are

SOURCES OF FUNDS

1. After-tax profit plus all noncash expenses such as depreciation and amortization
2. Decreases in an asset account (except a component of working capital)
3. Increases in a liability account (except a component of working capital)
4. Increases in an equity account (except the retained earnings account)

USES OF FUNDS

1. Increases in an asset account (except a component of working capital)
2. Decreases in a liability account (except a component of working capital
3. Payment of dividends
4. Decreases in an equity account (except the retained earnings account)

The principal recurring source of working capital is after-tax profits. The actual accounting concept used is the change in the balance in the retained earnings account. Note that the funds flow statement begins with after-tax profits, emphasizing the importance of income and its components in assessing the performance of the business operation.

Other sources of working capital include decreases in an asset account (other than current assets). This will result, for example, when fixed assets are sold. Unless a firm is in the business of selling machinery and equipment, any such transaction is considered nonrecurring and in many cases will reduce the firm's ability to generate revenue in the future.

The increase in a noncurrent liability account often represents an increase in long-term bank borrowing (an increase in the notes payable balance). Increases in an equity account are usually reflective of additional ownership investment (an increase in common stock or paid-in capital). In any case, these represent an additional source of funds.

Other uses of cash include the purchase of additional machinery and equipment and an increase in another noncurrent asset account. Decreases in a noncurrent liability account, such as the repayment of a long-term loan, are also included as a use of funds. The payment of dividends to shareholders and a proprietorship or partnership draw also fall into this category.

Table 2-3 presents the statement of changes in financial position for Deere for the year ending October 31, 1985. The information used in

TABLE 2-3. Statement of Changes in Financial Position for Deere for Year Ending October 31, 1985 (in thousands)

Working Capital Provided			
After-tax Profit	$ 30,505		
Plus depreciation	194,528		
Working capital from operations		$ 225,033	
Increase in long-term debt		135,602	
Increase in all other noncurrent liabilities		24,077	
Increase in common stock		39	
Increase in paid-in capital		5,120	
Total working capital provided			$ 389,871
Working Capital Applied			
Increase in gross fixed assets		$ 145,119	
Increase in all other noncurrent assets		21,571	
Decrease in deferred income tax		57,549	
Loss from sale of fixed assets		32,665	
Dividends paid		67,876	
Total working capital applied			324,780
Increase in working capital			$ 65,091
Net Change in Working Capital			
Increase (Decrease) in Current Assets			
Cash		$(541)	
Accounts receivable		(194,903)	
Inventory		(92,527)	
Prepaids		(48,075)	
			$(239,896)
Increase (Decrease) in Current Liabilities			
Accounts payable		$(98,862)	
Short-term notes payable		(47,213)	
Total accruals		(17,430)	
Current maturities—long-term debt		(141,482)	
			(304,987)
Increase in working capital			$ 65,091
Beginning working capital balance (year end 1984)			$ 1,455,797
Ending working capital balance (year end 1985)			$ 1,520,888

creating the statement came from the 1985 income statement and the 1984 and 1985 balance sheets.

This traditional presentation nets working capital provided against working capital applied to get the increase or decrease in working capital. Additional details are provided showing the breakdown in the net change in working capital. This is accomplished by summing the net change in each working capital account to arrive at the net change in total working capital.

The statement of changes in financial position is particularly helpful when used in conjunction with the other financial statements to show the liquidity and financial flexibility of a business enterprise. This method of presenting financial information offers a clear description of the actual sources of funds available to an enterprise and the manner in which they have been allocated over the last operating period.

As stated in the previous chapter, the FASB has ruled that effective July 15, 1988, all business entities must substitute a cash flow statement for the statement of changes in financial position. FASB 95 also requires a change in the format of the cash flow statement. It will be divided into three basic activities: operating, financing, and investing. The usefulness of the cash flow statement will be increased significantly by arranging the format according to type of activity instead of sources and uses. In this format, the operating, financing, and investing activities as well as their impact on cash flow can be delineated and understood.

TRADITIONAL APPROACH TO FINANCIAL ANALYSIS

Financial analysis can be a frustrating and confusing topic for those unprepared to deal with its subtleties. On the surface it appears simple and straightforward, with its explicit calculations and often quoted rules of thumb. What the unsuspecting analyst fails to realize is that even though the numbers are specific, their interpretation is not. In fact, there is disagreement not only in the meaning of ratio values but also in the exact method of calculation. Ask any five financial analysts how to calculate and interpret a given ratio, and there will be at least three answers to the former question and twice that many to the latter.

The main problem in using traditional ratio analysis is that it is an exercise in ambiguity. Aside from the issue of calculation and interpretation, seldom will a firm's financial data be completely positive or completely negative. The result is that the analyst is constantly dealing with firms that perform well in some areas and poorly in others. Thus, the investment or credit decision is always made with some degree of uncertainty.

The only way to analyze financial statements is to approach the task in a systematic manner. This means using all of the tools at one's disposal and relying on past experience (personal and universal) to serve as a guide in interpreting the results. Whether making a loan or other credit decision, examining customers, competitors, suppliers, or subcontractors, evaluating merger or acquisition candidates, or analyzing one's own company, the use of financial statement analysis is an essential ingredient in the success or failure of an enterprise.

To examine a set of financial statements systematically, arrange them in such a way that comparisons can be easily made. The steps in financial statement analysis are as follows:

1. Arrange the statements in a comparative format.
2. Present the statements in common size format.
3. Calculate a representative set of financial ratios.
4. Examine trends in the ratios, and compare them with industry standards.

Ratios are only as good as the financial data from which they are calculated. Unusual cost items, heavily depreciated equipment, or other specific accounting practices can have a significant effect on financial statement values, which in turn will affect the calculated ratios. For an expanded discussion of the tools and techniques used in financial analysis, see Maness (1988).

Comparative Financial Statements

The first step in analyzing financial statements is to organize the financial data into a comparative format.

For this purpose, three years of financial data for the Chrysler Corporation are presented in comparative format in Table 2-4. The key feature of this method of presenting financial statements is that the data are arranged so that changes and trends in the various categories can be easily recognized and quickly analyzed. Use of the comparative format will minimize the problems encountered in presenting and understanding data from financial statements, where categories are frequently added or deleted from year to year due to varying levels of activity.

The period chosen for presentation, from 1983 to 1985, represents pivotal years in the Chrysler turnaround story. After posting five consecutive years of losses, the company recorded a $701 million profit in 1983. It was also in this year that the final installment on the federally guaranteed $1.5 billion loan was made, 7 years ahead of schedule. During the next 2 years, the corporation continued its rise to respectability in the auto industry, posting profits of $2,380 and $1,635 million. Sales

TABLE 2-4. Chrysler Corporation Comparative Financial Statements (in millions)

Balance Sheet as of December 31	1983	1984	1985
Assets			
Cash	$ 112	$ 75	$ 148
Cash equivalents	958	1,625	2,650
Accounts receivable	291	332	208
Inventory	1,301	1,626	1,863
Prepaid expenses	92	322	446
Current Assets	$ 2,754	$ 3,980	$ 5,314
Gross fixed assets	6,353	7,617	9,957
Accumulated depreciation	(2,334)	(2,535)	(2,665)
Total Assets	$ 6,772	$ 9,063	$12,605
Liabilities and Net Worth			
Accounts payable	$ 1,940	$ 2,330	$ 2,700
Accruals	1,276	1,549	1,615
Taxes Payable	182	194	313
Current maturities long-term debt	56	43	102
Current Liabilities	$ 3,454	$ 4,116	$ 4,729
Long-term debt	1,522	1,122	2,665
Deferred income tax	432	497	392
All other noncurrent liabilities	0	22	605
Total Liabilities	$ 5,408	$ 5,757	$ 8,391
Preferred stock	225	0	0
Common stock	122	124	153
Paid-in capital	2,276	2,325	1,943
Treasury stock	(3)	(65)	(34)
Retained earnings	(1,255)	921	2,153
Total Liabilities and Net Worth	$ 6,772	$ 9,063	$12,605
Income Statement			
Net sales	$13,388	$19,717	$21,553
Cost of sales	10,861	15,528	17,468
Gross profit	$ 2,526	$ 4,189	$ 4,085
Operating expenses	$ 1,060	$ 1,255	$ 1,364
Depreciation and amortization	457	554	476
Operating profit	$ 1,009	$ 2,380	$ 2,245
Interest expense	$ 209	$ 132	$ 180
All other expenses (income)	(303)	(1,067)	(305)
Before-tax profit	$ 1,103	$ 3,314	$ 2,370
Income taxes	$ 402	$ 934	$ 735
After-tax profit	$ 701	$ 2,380	$ 1,635
Dividends	$ (117)	$ 121	$ 116

growth can be viewed as one of the reasons for the success. After a disappointing 7 percent decrease in sales in 1982, the firm recorded sales growth of 31, 48, and 8 percent over the next 3 years, respectively.

As impressive as these figures are, they do not tell the entire story of the Chrysler turnaround. The dramatic changes can only be seen clearly in the common-size statements.

Common-Size Financial Statements

The second step in the analysis of financial statements is to calculate common-size financial statements from the data. The format of the presentation is similar to that of the comparative financial statements. The difference is that the data entry for each balance sheet category is expressed as a percentage of total assets. The common-size income state-

TABLE 2-5. Chrysler's Common-Size Financial Statements (Percentages)

Balance Sheet as of December 31	1983	1984	1985	RMA
Assets				
Cash	15.79	18.76	22.19	8.50
Accounts receivable	4.30	3.76	1.65	17.70
Inventory	19.22	17.94	14.78	42.50
All other current assets	1.36	3.55	3.54	4.00
Current Assets	40.66	43.92	42.15	72.80
Fixed assets (net)	59.34	56.08	57.85	18.90
Total Assets	100.00	100.00	100.00	100.00
Liabilities and Net Worth				
Accounts payable	28.65	25.71	21.42	15.20
Accruals	18.84	17.09	12.81	10.90
Taxes payable	2.68	2.14	2.48	3.50
Current maturities long-term debt	0.82	0.47	0.81	2.00
Current Liabilities	51.00	45.41	37.52	48.60
Long-term debt	22.47	12.38	21.14	15.00
Deferred income tax	6.37	5.48	3.11	1.50
All other noncurrent liabilities	0.00	0.24	4.80	3.40
Net worth	20.16	36.48	33.44	31.60
Total Liabilities and Net Worth	100.00	100.00	100.00	100.00
	1983	*1984*	*1985*	*RMA*
Income Statement for Year				
Net sales	100.00	100.00	100.00	100.00
Cost of sales	81.13	78.75	81.04	79.20
Gross profit	18.87	21.25	18.96	20.80
Operating expenses	7.92	6.37	6.33	NA
Depreciation and amortization	3.41	2.81	2.21	NA
Operating profit	7.54	12.07	10.42	5.20
Interest expense	1.56	0.67	0.84	NA
All other expenses (income)	(2.26)	(5.41)	(1.42)	NA
Before-tax profit	8.24	16.81	11.00	3.80
Income taxes	3.00	4.74	3.41	NA
After-tax profit	5.24	12.07	7.59	NA

ment is generated by dividing each income statement category by total sales and expressing it as a percentage.

The common-size statements for Chrysler are shown in Table 2-5. The primary advantages of this method of presenting financial statements are that it facilitates comparisons with industry standards or other firms by adjusting for differences in asset size or sales volume, and it makes the comparison of data across firms and over time more meaningful.

With its 1983 financial statements, Chrysler is beginning to show signs of a conservatively run and financially sound company. *Quick assets* (cash plus cash equivalents and accounts receivable) increased from 20 percent of total assets to 24 percent between 1983 and 1985. Even more revealing is the firm's cash position—by 1985 Chrysler held over 22 percent of total assets in cash plus equivalents. Inventory holdings fell steadily over this period to less than 15 percent of total assets. As current assets overall have increased, current liabilities have fallen from 51 percent of total assets in 1983 to less than 38 percent in 1985.

Much of Chrysler's increased profitability can be traced to its low overall operating expenses. During the period operating expenses have fallen to less than 9 percent of sales, resulting in after-tax profit margins exceeding those of its industry rivals. This increased profitability is in turn translated into increased dividend capacity and increased shareholders' equity.

Traditional Ratio Analysis

One way to compare the various parts of a business is to calculate a representative set of financial ratios. Ratio analysis is an analytical technique used to establish relationships among income statement, balance sheet, and cash flow statement categories.

The ratios will be grouped into five categories: liquidity, asset utilization, coverage, leverage, and profitability. They are the five functional areas of a business that reveal the strengths and weaknesses of an operation. There are literally hundreds of possible ratios that could be used in a financial analysis. When examined individually or in small numbers, ratios can be misleading. If they are calculated in sufficient numbers and used in conjunction with other measures, however, they can be quite useful.

The text will use Chrysler data for the year 1985. Ratio values for 3 years of financial data, from 1983 to 1985, are presented in Table 2-6. The ratios are those that have comparable industry data available. Since comparative data are from Robert Morris Associates (RMA) *Annual Statement Studies*, ratios are calculated according to RMA definitions. See

TABLE 2-6. Chrysler's Financial Ratios with Industry Comparisons

| | Period Ending December 31 | | | |
	1983	1984	1985	RMA
Liquidity				
Current ratio	0.80	0.97	1.12	1.50
Quick ratio	0.39	0.49	0.64	0.50
Asset Utilization				
Sales/receivables	45.97	59.35	103.87	16.60
Cost of sales/inventory	8.35	9.55	9.38	4.60
Cost of sales/payables	5.60	6.67	6.47	13.10
Sales/working capital	−19.12	−145.19	36.89	9.40
Sales/net fixed assets	3.33	3.88	2.96	18.20
Sales/total assets	1.98	2.18	1.71	2.60
Coverage				
EBIT/interest	6.27	26.11	14.19	4.30
Cash flow/CMLTD	20.80	68.56	20.78	8.80
Leverage				
Debt ratio	79.84	63.52	66.56	68.40
Fixed/worth	2.94	1.54	1.73	0.50
Debt/worth	3.96	1.74	1.99	2.30
Profitability				
Gross profit margin	18.87	21.25	18.96	20.80
Net profit margin	8.24	16.81	11.00	3.80
Return on assets	10.35	26.26	12.97	NA
Return on equity	51.39	71.99	38.79	NA

Appendix 2A for a complete discussion of the method of calculation for each ratio.

Liquidity Ratios. The liquidity ratios that are commonly used include the *current* and *quick ratios*. Together they provide a measure of the margin of safety in paying short-term obligations should the value of current assets fall. They are, however, not measures of liquidity in the traditional sense of the term. In order to serve as liquidity measures, they would need to indicate the ease of converting current assets into cash. Based on a working capital definition of liquidity, the measures assume that current assets will be converted into cash at a rate that is sufficient to cover maturing current liabilities.

Current ratio. Chrysler's current ratio is 1.12, slightly below the industry median of 1.50. The ratio indicates that Chrysler would have to liquidate its current assets at 89 percent of their book value to repay its short-term obligations in full (1/1.12 = 0.89, or 89 percent).

Quick ratio or the acid test. At a value of 0.64, Chrysler's quick ratio or acid test is somewhat better than the industry median of 0.50. A value less than 1, however, indicates that the company is dependent on its ability to liquidate inventories or other current assets to pay off its short-term obligations. If accounts receivable can be converted into cash, the current liabilities can be paid off at a rate of 64 cents on the dollar without relying on the sale of inventories. This is an important considera- tion, since inventories tend to be the most illiquid of the short-term assets.

Asset Utilization Ratios.   Asset utilization ratios typically used in finan- cial analysis are often referred to as turnover ratios; they include receiv- ables, inventory, payables, working capital, fixed asset, and total asset turnover. In each case, the ratio is used to analyze a firm's efficiency in generating sales with the resource being examined. A significantly low turnover rate may indicate underutilized or idle assets. An exceptionally high turnover rate may show an insufficient asset base for the level of sales being generated.

Sales/receivables.   Chrysler's sales-to-receivables ratio is 103.62, com- pared with the industry median of 16.60. Chrysler's performance in this area is inconsistent with industry practices. Generally speaking, a sales- to-receivables ratio that is more than six times the industry median would be interpreted favorably. There are two major issues that should be considered, however, when comparing this ratio to the industry stan- dard. First, a company's practices regarding accounts receivable should be similar to those of other firms in the industry. In this case they are not. Chrysler sells most of its receivables to a financing subsidiary and as a result has only 1.65 percent of its assets in receivables, compared to 17.70 percent for the industry. Second, sales trends that differ substan- tially from historical experience or that of the industry make compari- sons difficult. A substantial increase in sales during the last 2 months of the year will result in a higher than normal accounts receivable balance and a lower than normal sales-to-receivable ratio.

Cost of sales/inventory.   Chrysler's inventory turnover rate is 9.38 times, compared with the industry median of 4.60 times. This ratio indicates that merchandise inventories are being turned into cash at a faster rate than those of the median industry operation. The absolute difference between the two ratios is somewhat deceptive. The best way to interpret this ratio is relative to the industry median. From this perspec- tive, Chrysler's inventories are turning over at twice the rate of the median industry firm.

Even though Chrysler seems to be doing relatively well in this area, it would probably be a sound idea to study the inventory patterns and merchandising decisions to determine the reason for the higher inventory turnover. One explanation that should be explored is the difference in inventory holdings as a percentage of total assets. Chrysler has only 14.78 percent of its assets in inventory, compared to 42.50 percent in the industry. Often this can mean inadequate inventories, stockouts, and lost sales.

Cost of sales / payables. Chrysler's payables turnover is less than half of that found in the industry, 6.47 times compared to 13.10 times. This is due in part to the fact that accounts payable makes up a greater percentage of total liabilities and net worth for Chrysler than for the median industry firm (21.42 versus 15.20 percent). A greater reliance on trade credit indicates that the company is more dependent on its suppliers as a source of spontaneous financing than the typical industry operation.

Sales / working capital. The sales-to-working-capital ratio measures how efficiently working capital is being used to generate sales. For Chrysler it indicates that the company is turning its working capital over 36.84 times, compared with 9.40 times for the typical industry operation. Since the ratio is significantly above the industry median, it indicates that Chrysler's operation is undercapitalized relative to the typical industry operation.

Sales / net fixed assets. Chrysler's fixed asset utilization ratio of 2.96 is significantly below the median industry operation's ratio of 18.20. This suggests an underutilization of fixed assets in generating sales.

Sales / total assets. Although total asset turnover is near the industry value, 1.71 compared with 2.60, the evidence is clear that Chrysler may have a problem in the area of asset utilization. All of the six turnover ratios discussed deviated significantly from the industry median. Management should make an effort to analyze this area carefully.

Coverage Ratios. The two coverage ratios calculated here are times interest earned and cash flow-to-current maturities of long-term debt. These ratios are used to identify firms that are relying heavily on debt to capitalize their operations. The lower the value of a coverage ratio, the more dependent a firm is on external sources of financing and the more limited its future funding options; that is, limited financial flexibility.

EBIT / interest. Interest coverage as measured by times interest earned is 12.47 times for Chrysler, compared to the industry median of 4.30 times. The earnings before interest and taxes (EBIT)-to-interest is above the industry median, indicating that Chrysler is covering interest charges with a good safety margin. As a result, the operation is more capable of taking on additional debt than is the median firm in the industry.

Cash flow / current maturities of long-term debt. The value of cash flow-to-current maturities of long-term debt (CMLTD) for Chrysler is 20.70

times, compared to the industry median of 8.80 times. The favorable value of this ratio is due to the extremely low value for current maturities in 1985 (0.61 percent versus 2.0 percent for the median firm). Taking into consideration the value of times interest earned, debt service is not a major concern for management. If the firm decided to borrow additional funds, it has the financial flexibility to do so.

Leverage Ratios. Leverage ratios often used in a financial analysis include the debt, fixed-to-worth, and debt-to-worth ratios. As a category, high values for these ratios indicate a high level of financial risk and a low degree of financial flexibility in future financing decisions.

Debt ratio. Chrysler's debt ratio is 66.57 percent, compared to the industry median of 68.40 percent. This means that Chrysler's creditors hold claim to a smaller percentage of the total assets than those of the median industry operation, although the difference is not significant. In other words, Chrysler's shareholders have supplied a larger proportion of the financing for the operation than would be expected in this industry. This ratio provides further evidence that the firm is in a good position to seek additional outside financing.

Fixed/worth. The fixed-to-worth ratio measures the relative investment in fixed assets. The value for Chrysler is 1.73, compared to 0.50 for the median firm in the industry. This indicates that Chrysler has 173 percent of shareholders' equity invested in fixed assets; the median industry firm has only 50 percent.

Debt/worth. With the industry median at 2.30, Chrysler's debt-to-worth ratio is 1.99. This is again indicative of a greater degree of financial flexibility than the typical operation. The ratio reflects that for every $1 the owners have invested in the company, the creditors have $1.99.

Profitability Ratios. The profitability ratios calculated in the financial analysis include gross profit margin, net profit margin, return on assets, and return on equity. When used in conjunction with one another, they indicate the ability of management to control all aspects of the business operation.

Gross profit margin. Chrysler's gross profit margin is slightly below the industry median, 18.95 percent versus 20.80 percent. This indicates that its pricing strategy, that is, markup, is in line with that of the industry.

Net profit margin. The net profit margin measures the after-tax profits as a percentage of sales. Chrysler's net profit margin is 7.59 percent, indicating that for every $1 in sales, the firm is making 7.59 cents net profit. RMA does not publish tax information, so there is no comparison with the industry for this ratio. There is some indication that Chrysler is doing somewhat better than the typical industry firm. Chrysler's before-tax profit margin is 11.00 percent, significantly above the industry median of 3.80 percent.

Return on assets. Return on assets (ROA) is calculated as an after-tax return. Chrysler's ROA is 12.97 percent. Once again there is no direct comparison with the industry. Chrysler's before-tax ROA of 18.80 percent, however, is almost double the industry median of 9.60 percent.

Return on equity. The return on equity (ROE) measures the return to the stockholders. Chrysler's stockholders enjoyed a 38.79 percent after-tax return in 1985. When interpreting this ratio, the level of risk should be carefully considered. A high ROE can be the result of a highly leveraged operation, even when the net profit margin is substandard.

This fact is made clear by establishing the relationship among the profitability ratios and other relevant turnover ratios discussed earlier. Figure 2-1 shows all the ratios that go into calculating return on equity, referred to as the duPont System (see also Patrone and duBois, 1981, and Van Voorhis, 1981).

The major components that establish the relationship are net profit margin, total asset turnover, and the debt ratio. From Figure 2-1, it is clear that the return on equity depends on the ability to manage the income statement categories that go into the calculation of net profit margin and total asset turnover.

The bottom left-hand side of the figure shows net sales of $21,553 million. Through a series of subtractions (expenses, interest, and taxes), the after-tax profit comes to $1,635 million. Dividing after-tax profit by net sales yields a net profit margin of 7.59 percent. This is interpreted to mean that stockholders as residual claimants receive a return of 7.59 cents from every dollar of sales.

The right-hand side of the figure shows the breakdown of total assets into current and noncurrent assets. Dividing net sales by total assets yields the total asset turnover of 1.71. In other words, each dollar of assets is used to generate $1.71 in net sales during the year. Return on assets is calculated by multiplying the net profit margin by total asset turnover. The equation for return on assets is

$$\text{Return on Assets} = \text{Net Profit Margin} \times \text{Total Asset Turnover}$$
$$= \frac{\text{After-Tax Profit}}{\text{Net Sales}} \times \frac{\text{Net Sales}}{\text{Total Assets}}$$
$$= 7.59 \text{ Percent} \times 1.71 \text{ Times} = 12.97 \text{ Percent}$$

Since assets turned over 1.71 times during the year, the net profit

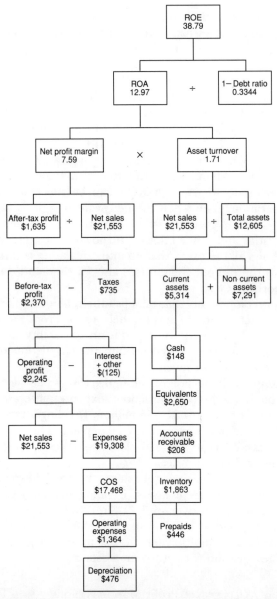

Figure 2-1. Return on equity ratio system applied to Chrysler, 1985. Dollar figures are in millions.

margin of 7.59 percent yields a return on assets of 12.97 percent. If total asset turnover is less than 1, ROA will be less than net profit margin, and vice versa. Note that a below-average net profit margin can be enhanced by an above-average total asset turnover to maintain an adequate return on assets.

Return on equity depends on ROA and the debt ratio. Thus, firms with the same ROA can have quite different ROEs, depending on the use of financial leverage. Highly leveraged firms will have, other things being equal, higher values for ROE and higher risk. The return on equity can be calculated by dividing return on assets by 1 minus the debt ratio (referred to as the equity ratio):

$$\text{Return on Equity} = \frac{\text{Return on Assets}}{\text{Equity Ratio}} = \frac{12.97 \text{ Percent}}{1 - 0.6657}$$

$$= \frac{12.97 \text{ Percent}}{0.3343} = 38.79 \text{ Percent}$$

The ability to keep stockholders content depends on the ability to generate a return on their invested capital. The increased use of financial leverage can turn an average ROA into an attractive ROE. There are actually three ways of increasing return on equity: increased profitability, better asset utilization, and increased leverage. Of the three, only increased leverage results in more risk; the other two result in increased return without increased risk. Thus, it is important to consider these three key areas when analyzing a firm's financial condition. Ignoring any one can give a distorted view of the operation or, more critically, can cause one to overlook details that are important in the overall analysis.

Analyzing Trends in Financial Ratios

Comparing a firm's performance with an industry benchmark is not the end of the analysis. It is also important to view the ratios within the context of their historical trends. In fact, trend analysis is in many ways a more important indicator of operating performance than are industry comparisons. Trend analysis is the only way to determine the direction of change in a firm's operations. It indicates if conditions are improving or getting worse.

It is important to distinguish between trends that are significant and those that are not. From data presented in Tables 2-5 and 2-6, trends in Chrysler's financial position can be determined.

Liquidity ratios, indicators of the firm's ability to meet short-term obligations as they come due, have increased steadily over the past 3 years. Although still below the industry standard, these accrual-based measures of liquidity indicate an improvement in short-term liquidity and less dependence on inventories to pay off short-term obligations. One reason that Chrysler's current and quick ratios seem to be giving mixed signals is the firm's low inventory holdings relative to total assets. The impact of this policy will become clearer as the other categories are analyzed.

In general, short-term asset utilization ratios are both better than industry comparisons and are steadily improving. Policies regarding working capital management are a contributing factor in the trend in these ratios. As receivables, inventory, and payables fall as a percentage of total assets, it is understandable that their respective asset turnover measures will increase in value. The relatively large investment in fixed assets and the resulting low values for fixed asset and total asset turnover, however, should be examined carefully. Management should determine whether the problem is with the operation or whether the industry comparisons are valid.

Chrysler has taken a very conservative approach to taking on more debt. As the percentage debt has varied, so has coverage. The figures using either measure of coverage jumped sharply in 1984 and returned to an intermediate level in 1985, but they are still above the industry standard.

This conservative approach to debt has resulted in a reduced reliance on short-term debt and only moderate use of long-term debt. As a result, the firm's leverage position has shown a steady improvement over the period. The fixed-to-worth ratio is still at a level above the comparison largely due to the higher than normal investment in fixed assets as defined by the comparison group.

Finally, over the past 3 years there has been a significant fluctuation in the profitability ratios. These fluctuations are due primarily to movements in profit margins and the debt ratio. In spite of these fluctuations, the profitability indicators reflect positively on the overall performance of management.

The *Valueline* stock rating service grades Chrysler's financial strength as a B. In terms of timeliness and safety of its stock, it rates average. Even though its share prices are a bit more volatile than the average share price in the market, Chrysler is better prepared than it has ever been to compete in the current economic environment. Taking all this into consideration, it is easy to adopt an optimistic attitude about the company's future.

SUMMARY

The traditional approach to financial analysis uses accrual-based measures. The basic accounting relationships, and the matching and realization principles, are used to record transactions and generate the financial statements used in financial analysis. The three basic financial statements are the income statement, balance sheet, and statement of changes in financial position. Accrual-based ratio analysis includes liquidity, asset utilization, coverage, leverage, and profitability ratios. Ratios are only general indicators of business performance. As such they can be enhanced by using cross-section and time-series comparisons.

Financial analysis is not a one-dimensional process. Accrual-based techniques, however, tend to focus on only one aspect of the operation – profitability. Although profitability is critical to an operation, it is important not to ignore other key aspects of financial health, namely, liquidity and financial flexibility.

REFERENCES

Chen, Kung H., and Thomas A. Shimerda. 1981. An Empirical Analysis of Useful Financial Ratios. *Financial Management* 10(1):51–60.

Maness, Terry S. 1988. *Introduction to Corporate Finance.* New York: McGraw-Hill Book Company.

Patrone, F.L., and Donald duBois. 1981. Financial Ratio Analysis for the Small Firm. *Journal of Small Business Management* 19(1):35–40.

RMA Annual Statement Studies. Various years. Philadelphia, PA: Robert Morris Associates.

Van Voorhis, Kenneth R. 1981. The duPont Model Revisited: A Simplified Approach to Small Business. *Journal of Small Business Management* 19(2):45–51.

APPENDIX 2A: FINANCIAL RATIOS

How many ratios to define and their methods of calculation are major issues when conducting a financial analysis. Calculating too few can lead to a biased look at the financial health of a firm; calculating too many can be cumbersome and redundant. A representative listing of ratios, grouped by the categories liquidity, asset utilization, coverage, leverage, and profitability is discussed here and summarized in Table 2A-1. To

TABLE 2A-1. Financial Ratios and Their Calculation

Ratio		Method of Calculation
Liquidity Ratios		
Current Ratio	=	$\dfrac{\text{Current Assets}}{\text{Current Liabilities}}$
Quick Ratio	=	$\dfrac{\text{Cash and Equivalents + Trade Receivables}}{\text{Total Current Liabilities}}$
Asset Utilization Ratios		
Sales/Receivables	=	$\dfrac{\text{Net Sales}}{\text{Trade Receivables}}$
Days Sales Outstanding	=	$\dfrac{365}{\text{Sales/Receivables}}$
Cost of Sales/Inventory	=	$\dfrac{\text{Cost of Sales}}{\text{Inventory}}$
Days Inventory	=	$\dfrac{365}{\text{Cost of Sales/Inventory}}$
Cost of Sales/Payables	=	$\dfrac{\text{Cost of Sales}}{\text{Payables}}$
Days Payable	=	$\dfrac{365}{\text{Cost of Sales/Payables}}$
Sales/Working Capital	=	$\dfrac{\text{Net Sales}}{\text{Net Working Capital}}$
Sales/Net Fixed Assets	=	$\dfrac{\text{Net Sales}}{\text{Net Fixed Assets}}$
Sales/Total Assets	=	$\dfrac{\text{Net Sales}}{\text{Total Assets}}$
Coverage Ratios		
EBIT/Interest	=	$\dfrac{\text{Earnings before Interest and Taxes}}{\text{Annual Interest Expense}}$
Cash Flow/CMLTD	=	$\dfrac{\text{Cash Flow}}{\text{Current Maturities of Long-Term Debt}}$
Leverage Ratios		
Debt Ratio	=	$\dfrac{\text{Total Liabilities}}{\text{Total Assets}}$
Fixed/Worth	=	$\dfrac{\text{Net Fixed Assets}}{\text{Tangible Net Worth}}$
Sales/Worth	=	$\dfrac{\text{Net Sales}}{\text{Tangible Net Worth}}$
Debt/Worth	=	$\dfrac{\text{Total Liabilities}}{\text{Tangible Net Worth}}$

TABLE 2A-1. (*Continued*)

Ratio		Method of Calculation
Profitability Ratios		
Gross Profit Margin	$=$	$\dfrac{\text{Gross Profit}}{\text{Net Sales}}$
Net Profit Margin	$=$	$\dfrac{\text{After-Tax Profit}}{\text{Net Sales}}$
EBIT/Total Assets	$=$	$\dfrac{\text{Earnings before Interest and Taxes}}{\text{Total Assets}}$
Return on Assets	$=$	$\dfrac{\text{After-Tax Profit}}{\text{Total Assets}}$
Return on Equity	$=$	$\dfrac{\text{After-Tax Profit}}{\text{Tangible Net Worth}}$

facilitate industry comparisons, most ratios are calculated using the Robert Morris Associates definitions as defined in *Annual Statement Studies*.

Liquidity Ratios

Accrual-based liquidity ratios are indicators of the ability of the operation to meet its current obligations as they mature. The resources available to meet current obligations are cash and assets that are easily converted into cash, such as marketable securities, inventory, and accounts receivable. These assets are found in the current assets section of the balance sheet. The dollar amount of current obligations is found in the current liabilities section of the balance sheet. They include accounts payable, accruals, short-term notes payable, and current maturities of long-term debt – obligations that by definition are due within 1 year.

Current Ratio. The current ratio is a commonly used indicator of short-term solvency. It reflects the ability to cover current liabilities out of current assets. The ratio is calculated by dividing current assets by current liabilities:

$$\text{Current Ratio} = \frac{\text{Current Assets}}{\text{Current Liabilities}}$$

The adequacy of this ratio depends on the type of business, the quality and distribution of the current assets, and the time of year. A current ratio of 2.0 may be more than adequate in one industry and totally inadequate in another. In addition, if a significant portion of accounts receivable is uncollectible or inventories are obsolete, a high current ratio will be misleading. Finally, comparing current ratios calculated at different times of the year when sales trends or inventory practices differ will lead to different results.

Quick Ratio or the Acid Test. The quick ratio or acid test examines the relationship between the most liquid current assets (cash, cash equivalents, and accounts and notes receivable) and total current liabilities. It represents a stricter measure of liquidity than the current ratio, focusing only on the most liquid current assets. To a limited extent, the quick ratio adjusts for the distribution of current assets by excluding inventories and other current assets from the calculation. This results in a more conservative measure of liquidity. The ratio is calculated by dividing cash and cash equivalents plus trade receivables by total current liabilities:

$$\text{Quick Ratio} = \frac{\text{Cash and Equivalents} + \text{Trade Receivables}}{\text{Total Current Liabilities}}$$

It is not unusual for an otherwise strong company to exhibit poor liquidity ratios. Substandard performance based on current and quick ratios may be due to a conscious policy of relying on current credit lines rather than cash balances to meet liquidity requirements. In this event, the underlying strength of the company will be clearly reflected in the values of its other ratios.

Asset Utilization Ratios

Asset utilization ratios are indicators of the ability to manage the assets of the firm effectively. They are designed to show the relationship between an income statement category (usually net sales) and a balance sheet category.

Sales/Receivables. The sales-to-receivables ratio, often referred to as the receivables turnover ratio, indicates the number of times accounts receivable turned over during an accounting period. It is calculated by dividing net sales by trade receivables (accounts receivable and notes receivable as a result of trade):

$$\text{Sales/Receivables} = \frac{\text{Net Sales}}{\text{Trade Receivables}}$$

A receivables turnover ratio that is greater than the industry median is generally a good indicator of a firm's management. There can, however, be a conceptual problem in comparing this ratio with the industry median if the firm has a significantly different percentage of total assets as accounts receivable. If all sales were cash sales (i.e., no credit sales and no accounts receivable), this ratio would have a value of infinity, which may not be a preferred position for a firm.

Days Sales Outstanding. Days sales outstanding (DSO), frequently referred to as the average collection period, indicates how long an average customer takes to pay for merchandise purchased. The ratio is actually the average number of days it takes to collect the accounts receivable balances. In general, as DSO increases, the likelihood of bad debt losses increases. Assuming a sales averaging period of 1 year, it is calculated by dividing 365 by the sales/receivables ratio:

$$\text{Days Sales Outstanding} = \frac{365}{\text{Sales/Receivables}}$$

A sales averaging period other than 1 year, for example 1 month, will require the calculation be made with 30 in the numerator and monthly sales in the denominator. The value of DSO should be consistent with the credit and collection policy of a company. The ratio shares the same bias as the sales-to-receivables ratio. Since there is no distinction made between cash sales and credit sales in its calculation, the ratio has a definite downward bias (just as sales/receivables has an upward bias). As long as the ratio of cash sales to credit sales is similar to that of the industry, however, the suggested method of calculation and interpretation is appropriate.

Cost of Sales/Inventory. The efficiency of inventory management is shown by the cost of sales-to-inventory ratio, often referred to as the inventory turnover ratio. It indicates the number of times the investment in inventory turns over during the accounting period (in most cases, 1 year). It is calculated by dividing cost of goods sold by inventory:

$$\text{Cost of Sales/Inventory} = \frac{\text{Cost of Sales}}{\text{Inventory}}$$

The calculation of this ratio assumes that sales are evenly divided during the months of the year and that inventory is readily marketable. The best way to interpret the cost of sales-to-inventory ratio is relative to the industry median, since the absolute difference between those two ratios may be somewhat deceptive.

There are two additional problems involved with the cost of sales-to-inventory ratio. One is a problem in calculation; the other is a problem in analysis. In calculating this ratio, there is some question as to the proper value for inventory. Is it year-ending inventory or an average inventory (beginning plus ending divided by 2 or a monthly summation divided by 12)? Once again, the choice is somewhat dictated by the industry comparison data available. As long as inventory management procedures are similar, the ratio should be calculated in the same manner as the comparison figures.

The analysis problem is a bit more complex. There can be two possible interpretations for any one value of this ratio. A high value may mean a good choice of inventory stock resulting in a high degree of liquidity. On the other hand, it may indicate that inventory is too small relative to sales, resulting in frequent stock-outs and loss of sales.

A low value for the ratio may indicate inventory levels that are too high relative to the level of sales or possibly inventory that is obsolete or in some other way not fit for sale. The same low value might also be the result of a conscious decision by management to increase the level of inventories for some well-defined reason, such as projected shortages in raw materials or an increase in expected future demand.

Days Cost of Goods Sold in Inventory (Days Inventory). The days cost of goods sold in inventory ratio, also called days' inventory, is a measure of the average number of days that inventory items are in stock. Assuming an annual sales averaging period, it is calculated by dividing 365 by the cost of sales-to-inventory ratio:

$$\text{Days Inventory} = \frac{365}{\text{Cost of Sales/Inventory}}$$

Values for this ratio vary considerably across industries. Inventory may turn over an average of once every 90 days in a large department store and an average of once every 20 days in a grocery store. Although there is a great deal of variation across industries, the ratio is a useful measure when examined within a firm over time or compared across firms within the same industry.

Cost of Sales/Payables. Cost of sales-to-payables is the third important turnover ratio used to track management's use of working capital. It looks at the number of accounts payable turns during the accounting period (in most cases, 1 year). It is calculated by dividing cost of sales by accounts payable:

$$\text{Cost of Sales/Payables} = \frac{\text{Cost of Sales}}{\text{Payables}}$$

A greater reliance on trade credit results in an increased level of risk for unsecured creditors.

Days Payable. The days payable ratio measures the number of days a company takes to pay for its inventory purchases. The value of this ratio should be in line with the terms offered by trade creditors. It is calculated by dividing the number of days in an accounting period (in most cases, 365) by the cost of sales-to-payables ratio:

$$\text{Days Payable} = \frac{365}{\text{Cost of Sales/Payables}}$$

Sales/Working Capital. The sales-to-working capital ratio measures how effectively current resources are being used in the operating activities of a firm; that is, how well the firm is generating net sales. A relatively low ratio is indicative of underutilized working capital; a relatively high ratio often points to undercapitalization, which leaves unsecured creditors unnecessarily exposed. The ratio is calculated by dividing net sales by net working capital (current assets minus current liabilities):

$$\text{Sales/Working Capital} = \frac{\text{Net Sales}}{\text{Net Working Capital}}$$

If this ratio is significantly above the industry median, the operation is undercapitalized relative to the typical industry operation, and vice versa.

Sales/Net Fixed Assets. Fixed asset utilization, or fixed asset turnover, is the first of two ratios measuring the ability to manage a firm's long-term assets. Sales-to-net fixed assets is calculated by dividing net sales by net fixed assets (plant and equipment less accumulated depreciation):

$$\text{Sales/Net Fixed Assets} = \frac{\text{Net Sales}}{\text{Net Fixed Assets}}$$

A fixed asset utilization ratio that is below the median industry operation suggests an underutilization of fixed assets in generating sales. Additionally, the analyst should be aware that there are several conceptual problems in interpreting this ratio. Differences in accounting practices, use of leased equipment, or differences in the labor intensity of the operation can cause difficulty in comparing it across firms. If the book value of fixed assets seriously understates their market value (caused by accelerated methods of depreciating equipment for tax purposes or inflation), significant differences in the ratio between new operations and older, established operations will arise. Reliance on operating leases for capital equipment instead of actual ownership provides an upward bias to this ratio. Additionally, if the operation varies sharply from the industry in terms of labor utilization, its asset turnover ratio is also likely to vary.

Sales/Total Assets. The sales-to-total assets ratio is a measure of total asset utilization or total asset turnover. It provides information on the effectiveness of the use of the firm's total assets in generating sales. The ratio is calculated by dividing net sales by total assets:

$$\text{Sales/Total Assets} = \frac{\text{Net Sales}}{\text{Total Assets}}$$

Coverage Ratios

Coverage ratios measure a firm's ability to service its debt – interest charges plus principal amortization. They indicate the number of times fixed debt charges are covered out of operations.

EBIT/Interest. A firm's ability to meet its annual interest expense is measured by the EBIT-to-interest ratio, often called times interest earned. It is calculated by dividing earnings before interest and taxes by annual interest expense:

$$\text{EBIT/Interest} = \frac{\text{Earnings before Interest and Taxes}}{\text{Annual Interest Expense}}$$

When this ratio is below the industry median, the firm may be experiencing difficulties in adequately covering interest charges. As a result, the operation is less capable of taking on additional debt than is the median firm in the industry. The opposite is true if the ratio is above the industry median.

Cash Flow/Current Maturities of Long-Term Debt. The cash flow-to-current maturities of long-term debt ratio measures the extent to which the principal on debt is covered by cash flow. Since cash flow from operations is the primary source of repayment of debt, this ratio indicates the firm's ability to service the current portion of its long-term debt obligations. It is calculated by dividing cash flow by current maturities of long-term debt:

$$\text{Cash Flow/CMLTD} = \frac{\text{Cash Flow}}{\text{Current Maturities of Long-Term Debt}}$$

Following RMA's calculation of this ratio, cash flow is defined as profit after taxes plus depreciation, depletion, and amortization expense. A favorable value for the ratio may be due to a low value for current maturities. The ratio should be interpreted in light of the value of times interest earned.

Leverage Ratios

Leverage ratios are closely related to coverage ratios. They measure the extent to which a firm is capitalized through debt. Highly leveraged companies will have higher values for coverage ratios. A heavy reliance on debt sources to finance a business is common for new ventures. Firms that are highly leveraged are more vulnerable to downturns in business activity and have a higher degree of risk associated with their operations.

Debt Ratio. The debt ratio measures creditors' claims against total assets relative to total claims. It serves as an indicator of the unsecured creditors' margin of safety in the event of a business downturn or liquidation. The higher the ratio, the greater the risk to creditors. The debt ratio is calculated by dividing total liabilities by total assets:

$$\text{Debt Ratio} = \frac{\text{Total Liabilities}}{\text{Total Assets}}$$

By taking the reciprocal of the debt ratio (1/debt ratio), an analyst can determine the number of times the book value of assets covers liabilities. For example, if the debt ratio is 0.40, the book value of assets is 2.5 times greater than total liabilities. Asset values would have to fall over 60 percent before a company would be considered insolvent.

A value for this ratio that is smaller than the industry comparison indicates that shareholders hold claim to a much greater percentage of the total assets than those of the median industry operation. In this case, shareholders have supplied a much larger proportion of the financing for the operation than would be expected in the industry. When liabilities are a smaller than normal percentage of total assets, creditors tend to have a greater degree of confidence in management's ability to control the firm's debt. By maintaining a high degree of creditor confidence, owners would be in a much better position to seek additional outside financing.

Fixed/Worth. The fixed-to-worth ratio measures the relative degree to which owners have invested their equity in fixed assets (plant and equipment). The higher this ratio, the more vulnerable are creditors in the event of a company liquidation. The lower the ratio the better the cushion if such an event should occur. The ratio is calculated by dividing net fixed assets (gross fixed assets less accumulated depreciation) by tangible net worth (total net worth minus intangibles):

$$\text{Fixed/Worth} = \frac{\text{Net Fixed Assets}}{\text{Tangible Net Worth}}$$

A heavy use of operating leases for capital equipment (not shown on the balance sheet) will tend to lower this ratio. If the operation had no leased equipment whereas the typical industry operation has a significant amount (as evidenced by the percentage of sales-to-lease and rental expense), the creditors' cushion would be relatively better than the comparison indicates.

Sales/Worth. When the fixed-to-worth ratio is multiplied by the sales-to-net fixed assets ratio, the resulting ratio is called the trading ratio. Sales-to-worth ratio measures the extent to which a firm's sales volume is supported by equity capital. A high value is indicative of a heavy debt burden and an operation that is dependent on continued favorable internal and external conditions. A relatively low value indicates the firm has either excess resources or inadequate sales for the level of invested capital. This ratio is calculated by dividing net sales by tangible net worth:

$$\text{Sales/Worth} = \frac{\text{Net Sales}}{\text{Tangible Net Worth}}$$

A relatively high trading ratio indicates that the ownership equity is inadequate relative to the sales volume; that is, the firm is overtrading. An extremely low value indicates that ownership equity is not being adequately used to generate sales.

Debt/Worth. The debt-to-worth ratio shows the relative ownership claims of creditors compared with those of owners. A low value indicates a low level of financial risk and a great degree of flexibility in future financing decisions. A high ratio indicates exactly the opposite. The ratio is calculated by dividing total liabilities by tangible net worth:

$$\text{Debt}/\text{Worth} = \frac{\text{Total Liabilities}}{\text{Tangible Net Worth}}$$

The interpretation of this ratio is similar to that of the debt ratio. In fact, the debt-to-worth ratio (D/E) is simply an algebraic transformation of the debt-to-asset ratio (D/A):

$$\frac{D}{A} = \frac{D}{D+E} = \frac{D/E}{1+D/E}$$

and

$$\frac{D}{E} = \frac{D}{A-D} = \frac{D/A}{1-D/A}$$

The debt-to-asset ratio will vary within its limits of 0 to 100 percent, whereas the debt-to-worth ratio will vary between 0 and infinity. Generally speaking, owners should have more invested in a business than creditors. In many situations, analysts consider a value for the debt-to-worth ratio greater than 1 unsafe. In any event, the larger the ratio the more vulnerable the position of the firm's creditors and the more limited the firm in securing additional external debt without first securing an additional equity injection. In the event of a highly liquid operation, this statement may not hold true. A firm possessing high-quality current assets along with a high value for its current ratio can operate safely with a higher debt-to-worth ratio.

Profitability Ratios

Profitability ratios are often used to evaluate overall management performance. The ratios discussed so far are indicative of the type of job management is doing; the profitability ratios reflect two important aspects of a firm's operations that have not been examined. First, they show whether the expense structure of an operation is appropriate for the level of sales generated. Second, they express the profitability of the operation relative to the level of resource investment.

Gross Profit Margin. The gross profit margin, an income statement ratio, is calculated by dividing gross profit (net sales minus cost of sales) by net sales:

$$\text{Gross Profit Margin} = \frac{\text{Gross Profit}}{\text{Net Sales}}$$

The difference between the gross profit margin of the firm being studied and that of the median industry firm indicates different product pricing practices. As is often the case, firms experiencing financial difficulties will engage in price competition to boost sales, thus lowering gross profit margin. As a firm turns around, this strategy should be carefully reevaluated.

Net Profit Margin. The net profit margin measures after-tax profits as a percentage of sales. It is calculated by dividing profit after tax by net sales:

$$\text{Net Profit Margin} = \frac{\text{After-Tax Profit}}{\text{Net Sales}}$$

The *Annual Statement Studies* does not publish a comparison figure for net profit margin; however, it does publish the before-tax profit margin. Comparisons can be made with before-tax values; however, care should be taken in generalizing such comparisons.

EBIT/Total Assets. The ratio of operating profit to total assets, that is, the basic earning power of assets, measures the effectiveness in generating profit from total assets. It is calculated by dividing EBIT by total assets:

$$\text{EBIT/Total Assets} = \frac{\text{Earnings before Interest and Taxes}}{\text{Total Assets}}$$

This ratio examines the effective use of assets in generating profit regardless of the manner in which the operation is capitalized or the firm's specific tax situation. By using EBIT (operating profit), one is able to determine the basic ability of the operation to generate profit. Firms with the same basic earning power but different degrees of financial leverage will earn vastly different returns for shareholders.

Return on Assets. ROA measures the ability to generate after-tax profit out of a given total asset base. Return on assets is calculated by dividing after-tax profit by total assets:

$$\text{Return on Assets} = \frac{\text{After-Tax Profit}}{\text{Total Assets}}$$

RMA data do not provide tax information for comparisons. Thus, when using this database for comparison, there is no way to generate industry averages for after-tax ratios.

Return on Equity. ROE measures the return to stockholders. As a general measure of operating efficiency, it shows management's capacity to translate shareholder equity into profit within the business operating environment. It is calculated by dividing after-tax profit by tangible net worth:

$$\text{Return on Equity} = \frac{\text{After-Tax Profit}}{\text{Tangible Net Worth}}$$

When ROE is too low, it is difficult for a firm to attract equity funds for expansion. This in turn makes it more difficult to engage in long-term borrowing, especially if the firm's leverage position is also weak. No operation can hope to survive and adequately provide for future growth without generating a return for its stockholders.

One word of caution: Extreme care should be exercised when interpreting this ratio. A high return could be the result of an undercapitalized firm coupled with a substandard profit (measured by the net profit margin) rather than an efficiently run operation.

SUMMARY

The temptation to adhere strictly to a set of industry norms should be avoided, since expecting a firm's ratios to fall within a certain range can result in misclassification. Differences in asset structure, physical location, number of years in operation, size, product diversification, and other factors make each firm unique. Any one of these factors can cause ratios to vary legitimately from industry norms.

Ratio analysis is an important tool in financial analysis. When used in conjunction with other measures of financial health, for example, cash flow analysis, it helps identify strengths and weaknesses in the financial position of a firm. In addition to industry comparisons, it is important to view the ratios within the context of their historical trends. This is evident when analyzing a firm such as International Harvester, which has recently gone through a difficult period. Within its historical context, ratios that are currently below industry levels reveal improved conditions that point to better times to come.

APPENDIX 2B: CHOOSING REPRESENTATIVE RATIOS FOR ANALYSIS

Financial ratio analysis is a key ingredient in determining the operating performance and financial condition of a business enterprise. But with literally hundreds of available ratios, most analysts have a difficult time determining which should be calculated and which can be omitted without significant loss in information.

Chen and Shimerda (1981) examined this issue by studying the most frequently used ratios in the finance and accounting literature. As a result of their study, they grouped the ratios into seven categories, or factors, based on the degree of common information contained in each.

Principal Components Analysis

Chen and Shimerda began by looking at 26 empirical studies analyzing 65 financial ratios. Their goal was to eliminate the overlapping of information and determine a manageable set of ratios.

Using the statistical tool principal components analysis, they developed an empirically based classification scheme to group ratios into meaningful categories. The technique summarizes interrelationships among the ratios and groups them into a reduced set of factors that retains a majority of the information (variance). Ratios classified by the same factor are highly correlated with one another, in many cases using the same data in their calculations. Instead of calculating every ratio in the category, one is chosen as the representative ratio. It contains the majority of information represented by all the ratios in the category.

The seven categories identified in the study and the ratios that showed the highest correlation within each are listed in Table 2B-1.

Most of the ratios were discussed in Chapter 2. Those that were not can, in most cases, be read off the common-size statements or be calculated by combining ratios that were discussed.

Ratios with total assets in the denominator can be found in the common-size statements. These include current assets/total assets, long-

TABLE 2B-1. Financial Ratio Categories and Correlated Ratios

Return on Investment
* Return on equity
  Return on assets
  Operating profit/total assets
  Operating profit/sales
  Capital Intensiveness
* Current assets/total assets
  Sales/total assets
  Sales/worth
  Inventory Intensiveness
  Sales/working capital
  Current assets/sales
* Sales/inventory
  Financial Leverage
  Debt ratio
* Debt/worth
  Net worth/total assets
  Long-term debt/total assets
  Receivables Intensiveness
  Receivables/inventory
* Sales/receivables
  Short-Term Liquidity
* Current ratio
  Quick ratio
  Current assets/total assets
  Cash Position
  Cash/sales
* Cash/total assets
  Cash/current assets

*Representative set of ratios. See text for explanation of how they were derived.

term debt/total assets, net worth/total assets, and cash/total assets. Current assets/sales and cash/sales are simply familiar ratios combined with sales/total assets. Only three ratios – receivables/inventory, sales/inventory, and cash/current liabilities – are unusual.

The similarity of each ratio with the factor is measured by its loading factor, statistically representing the correlation coefficient of the ratio with the factor. Since loading factors varied from study to study, they are not reported. All ratios listed in each category, however, showed significantly strong loading factors with the category.

Identifying ratio categories is only the first step in reducing the number of ratios to calculate in a financial analysis. A problem that still exists is that there is no satisfactory procedure to choose the appropriate ratio to represent each category.

Selection of the most representative ratio is still an ad hoc procedure. The best thing to do is choose the one that has most of the common information (determined by the ratio with the highest loading factor) and eliminates most of the overlapping information. Based on these criteria, ratios marked with an asterisk in Table 2B-1 are the representative ones. Those seven ratios provide from 75 to 80 percent of the information represented by all 65 ratios.

Chapter 3

Cash Flow Statement

When examining the profitability of a business operation, the traditional ratio approach provides an analyst with the necessary information to complete the task. But, as discussed in Chapter 2, a major problem with the ratio approach is its lack of a clear measure of liquidity. The reason for this weakness is twofold: (1) Most accrual-based liquidity measures use a working capital definition of funds, and (2) firms use cash rather than working capital to pay financial obligations.

Cash flow analysis has been suggested as the solution to this analytical weakness (see Maness and Henderson, 1985). But there is a dilemma with cash flow analysis: Even though it is widely used and an integral part of the external reporting requirements of a firm, many users of financial data do not understand the cash flow statement or have only a general idea of the information presented in it. The FASB *Statement of Financial Accounting Standards No. 95*, "Statement of Cash Flows" (1987), however, has cleared up several issues that have long troubled users of the cash flow statement, namely, the purpose of the statement, the proper definition of funds, and the statement format.

CASH FLOW STATEMENT

The primary purpose of the cash flow statement is to provide information on the cash receipts and cash payments of a business operation during a specified time period. The statement presents cash flow data on a firm's operating, investing, and financing activities. Those who use financial information — investors, creditors, and financial analysts — will find the cash flow data helpful in assessing future cash flows, determining the relationship between net income and cash flow, and evaluating the ability of an entity to pay dividends, service its debt, and finance growth from internal operations.

The arrangement of the cash flow statement into operating activities, investing activities, and financing activities differs significantly from the arrangement of the statement of changes in financial position into sources and uses of funds. Cash flow information grouped by activity is more valuable for prediction purposes because it matches inflows and outflows within each activity and makes it easier to identify related transactions within each category.

Activity Format

Grouping the activities of a firm into operating, financing, and investing is a more meaningful way to categorize cash flows. The Financial Accounting Standards Board has provided specific guidelines for this purpose, although there is still a great degree of flexibility in how transactions are classified into these activities. The exact definition of certain items depends on the specific nature of the individual business operation.

FASB 95 provides a set of guidelines to help classify cash receipts and cash payments according to type of activity. Using these guidelines, operating activities is a residual category encompassing everything that is not classified as an investing or financing activity. Table 3-1 presents the general guidelines for the suggested classification scheme.

The purpose of this classification scheme is to combine transactions with similar characteristics and to separate transactions with dissimilar characteristics. Grouping activities in this way enables analysts to identify significant relationships within each category and evaluate an entity's ability to meet its financial obligations. In the end, the change in cash plus cash equivalents is the net change reported.

Investing Activities. An *investing activity* relates to transactions that involve the acquisition, disposition, and retirement of property, plant, and equipment or other productive assets, the lending of money and collecting on those loans, or the acquiring and disposing of equity instruments. This section includes only cash transactions. Noncash transactions completed with debt or equity securities are reported in a related disclosure that may take the form of a written statement or a tabular schedule. Securing assets by assuming directly related liabilities such as a mortgage to the seller or a capital lease are examples of noncash transactions.

Productive assets are those that are expected to generate revenues over a long period of time. Securities disclosed under this activity are short- and long-term investments representing ownership interests in controlled companies. Highly liquid securities that are considered cash equivalents, such as money market funds, certificates of deposit, and treasury bills with maturities of less than 90 days, however, are not included. Transac-

TABLE 3-1.   Classification Scheme for Identifying Activities as Operating, Investing, or Financing

Operating Activities
Inflows of Cash
  Receipts from customers for the sale of goods
  Receipts from customers for the provision of services
  Interest receipts on loans
  Dividend receipts on equity securities
Outflows of Cash
  Payments to suppliers (acquisition of inventory)
  Payments to employees (services)
  Payments to suppliers (other goods and services)
  Payments of interest to lenders and other creditors
  Payments to government (taxes, duties, fines, fees)
Investing Activities
Inflows of Cash
  Receipts from loans (principal collected from another business entity)
  Receipts from the sale of loans to another entity
  Receipts from the sale of debt or equity securities of other business entities (other than cash equivalents)
  Receipts from the sale of property, plant, and equipment and other productive assets
Outflows of Cash
  Loans made to other business entities
  Loans purchased from other business entities
  Payments to acquire debt or equity securities of other business entities (other than cash equivalents)
  Payments to acquire property, plant, and equipment and other assets
Financing Activities
Inflows of Cash
  Proceeds from the issuance of equity securities
  Proceeds from the issuance of debt (bonds, mortgages, notes, and other short- and long-term instruments)
Outflows of Cash
  Payments of dividends or other distributions to shareholders
  Payments to repurchase stock of the entity
  Payments of debt (principal amounts)

tions in such instruments are treated as part of the cash management function of the business and thus defined as cash.

Investing activities that generate cash include the collection of loans, the sale of debt instruments or equity securities of other business entities, the sale of long-lived productive assets, and the sale of other assets such as another business entity. If, however, such an asset is acquired with the intention of renting it to other entities for a short period of time and then selling it, the activity would be classified an operating activity in the same manner as any other inventory transaction.

Uses of cash in this category include loans made or purchased and payments to acquire assets such as debt or equity securities of other entities and long-lived productive assets.

Financing Activities. *Financing activities* include all transactions that relate to acquiring and servicing outside capital from creditors and investors. Transactions involving creditors include borrowing money and repaying debts or otherwise retiring those loans. Transactions involving investors include selling or repurchasing stock and paying dividends. Surprisingly, interest payments are excluded. The FASB treats interest expense as part of operations because interest is reported on the income statement, that is, the statement of operations.

Operating Activities. All activities that are not specifically included as investing or financing activities are considered *operating activities*. These activities are transactions and events that normally affect the income statement. They include all activities concerned with providing goods and services to customers and thus comprise the day-to-day operations of a business enterprise.

Cash inflows are all receipts from customers for goods and services and interest and dividends received from loans and investments. They include all cash receipts that do not originate from transactions defined as investing or financing activities. Cash outflows are payments to suppliers, employees, and the government. They include all cash payments that do not originate from transactions defined as investing or financing activities. For a more analytical discussion of operating activities, see Drtina and Largay (1985) or Gombola and Ketz (1981).

Cash Flow Format

There are two principal formats for reporting cash flow from operating activities: the direct method and the indirect method. Although the FASB has specified that the direct format is the preferred method, most users are more familiar with the indirect format. Thus, most cash flow statements will likely be presented using the indirect format.

Cash Flows from Operating Activities: The Indirect Approach. The *indirect format*, often referred to as the *reconciliation method*, is the most widely used method of presentation for external reporting (Seed, 1984). Firms must adjust net income so as to report the same net cash flow from operations as determined by the direct method. The cash flow statement prepared by the indirect approach begins with net income and adjusts for items that do not result in current-period cash transactions. This method of calculation backs into net cash flow from operations by removing the effects of accruals and deferrals that result in revenues and expenses but do not generate or use cash and by adjusting for operating receipts and expenditures of cash that do not result in revenues or expenses. Examples of these adjustments are depreciation, depletion, and amortization expense; deferred taxes and prepaids; and changes in accounts receivable, inventory, accounts payable, and other current liabilities, including accruals.

Table 3-2 illustrates the cash flow statement using the indirect method. Financial data are from Deere (see Chapter 2). Net income is adjusted for transactions that did not result in current-period cash receipts or outlays. The first step is to add back depreciation and amortization. The next adjustment requires subtracting the increase in current asset accounts: accounts receivable, inventory, and other current assets. If the balances in the accounts decreased, the amounts would be added instead of subtracted. Next, any increases in current liability accounts — accounts payable and accrued and deferred taxes — are added (decreases are subtracted). The result is net cash flow from operations.

Cash Flows from Operating Activities: The Direct Approach. The direct cash flow presentation computes cash inflows and cash outflows directly, showing the major components of operating cash receipts and operating cash disbursements. A cash flow statement prepared in the *direct format* closely resembles a condensed cash-basis income statement. For example, it begins with cash received from customers and subtracts cash paid out to suppliers and employees.

The direct approach to the calculation of net cash flow from operations for Deere is shown in Table 3-3. It begins with the derivation of cash provided by operating activities. The first step is to determine the cash received from customers. This is done by adjusting sales for changes in the accounts receivable balance (subtracting increases or adding decreases) as follows:

Net sales	$4,399,168	$4,060,648
Plus (minus)		
Decrease (increase) in accounts receivable	(197,526)	194,903
Cash received from customers	$4,201,642	$4,255,551

A sale will not add to a firm's cash balances unless funds are actually collected. Net cash inflows result from cash sales in the current period plus collections of credit sales from prior periods. To the extent that the balance of accounts receivable increases, current period sales are greater than actual cash inflows. Likewise, a decrease in the accounts receivable balance indicates that cash inflows are actually greater than current

TABLE 3-2. Deere's Cash Flow Statements: Indirect Method (000)

	Period Ending October 31	
	1984	1985
Cash Flows from Operating Activities		
Net Income	$ 104,944	$ 30,505
Noncash items included in operating profit		
Plus depreciation and amortization	203,091	194,528
Plus (minus)		
Decrease (increase) in accounts receivable	(197,526)	194,903
Decrease (increase) in inventory	92,600	92,527
Decrease (increase) in other current assets	58,504	(1,034)
Increase (decrease) in accounts payable	17,940	(98,862)
Increase (decrease) in accrued taxes	45,093	(17,426)
Increase (decrease) in deferred taxes	(76,587)	(57,549)
Net Cash Flow from Operations	$ 248,059	$ 337,592
Cash Flows from Investing Activities		
Plus (minus)		
Decrease (increase) in gross fixed assets	(1,241)	(145,119)
Accumulated depreciation (sold)	(79,641)	(32,665)
Decrease (increase) in other noncurrent assets	(66,632)	(21,571)
Cash Flow (Used) Provided in Investing Activities	$(147,514)	$(199,355)
Cash Flows from Financing Activities		
Plus new borrowing		
Short-term notes payable	$ 567,783	$ 520,570
Long-term debt	0	154,253
(Minus) debt payments		
Short-term notes payable	(712,186)	(567,783)
Current maturities long-term debt	(9,244)	(157,833)
Additional long-term debt amortization	(50,277)	0
Plus (minus)		
Increase (decrease) in other noncurrent liabilities	19,881	21,777
Increase (decrease) in common stock	79	39
Increase (decrease) in paid-in capital	(22,294)	5,120
Increase (decrease) in dividends payable	20	(4)
Adjustments to retained earnings	(96)	(56)
(Minus) dividends paid	(67,772)	(67,820)
Cash Flow Provided (Used) in Financing Activities	$(274,106)	$ (91,737)
Net Increase (Decrease) in Cash and Equivalents	$(173,561)	$ 46,500
Cash and Cash Equivalents at Beginning of Year	214,884	41,323
Cash and Cash Equivalents at End of Year	$ 41,323	$ 87,823

period sales. In other words, collections of previous period sales were greater than current period sales uncollected. This is the rationale behind the receivables adjustment in the calculation of operating cash receipts.

TABLE 3-3. Deere's Cash Flow Statements: Direct Method (000)

	Period Ending October 31	
	1984	1985
Cash Flows from Operating Activities		
Cash received from customers	$4,201,642	$4,255,551
Plus refundable income taxes	58,504	(1,034)
Plus other operating income	237,058	205,575
Cash provided by operating activities	$4,497,204	$4,460,092
Cash paid to suppliers and employees	$4,012,742	$3,897,606
Plus interest expense	234,609	199,320
Plus other operating expenses	6,223	15,097
Plus income taxes paid	(4,429)	10,477
Cash disbursed for operating activities	$4,249,145	$4,122,500
Net Cash Flow from Operations	$ 248,059	$ 337,592
Cash Flows from Investing Activities		
Plus (minus)		
Decrease (increase) in gross fixed assets	(1,241)	(145,119)
Accumulated depreciation (sold)	(79,641)	(32,665)
Decrease (increase) in other noncurrent assets	(66,632)	(21,571)
Cash Flow (Used) Provided in Investing Activities	$ (147,514)	$ (199,355)
Cash Flows from Financing Activities		
Plus new borrowing		
Short-term notes payable	$ 567,783	$ 520,570
Long-term debt	0	154,253
(Minus) debt amortization		
Short-term notes payable	(712,186)	(567,783)
Current maturities long-term debt	(9,244)	(157,833)
Additional long-term debt amortization	(50,277)	0
Plus (minus)		
Increase (decrease) in other noncurrent liabilities	19,881	21,777
Increase (decrease) in common stock	79	39
Increase (decrease) in paid-in capital	(22,294)	5,120
Increase (decrease) in dividends payable	20	(4)
Adjustments to retained earnings	(96)	(56)
(Minus) dividends paid	(67,772)	(67,820)
Cash Flow Provided (Used) in Financing Activities	$(274,106)	$ (91,737)
Net Increase (Decrease) in Cash and Equivalents	$ (173,561)	$ 46,500
Cash and Cash Equivalents at Beginning of Year	214,884	41,323
Cash and Cash Equivalents at End of Year	$ 41,323	$ 87,823

The next step is to calculate cash disbursed for operating activities. Cash paid to suppliers and employees is calculated by adjusting cost of goods sold for changes in inventories (adding increases and subtracting decreases), accounts payable, and other current liabilities (subtracting increases or adding decreases for each of these two accounts). Finally, operating expenses adjusted for changes in prepaids and accruals [adding increases (subtracting decreases) in prepaids and subtracting increases (adding decreases) in accruals] as follows:

Cost of sales	$3,598,204	$3,355,318
Plus (minus)		
Increase (decrease) in inventory	(92,600)	(92,527)
Decrease (increase) in payables	(17,940)	98,862
Plus operating expenses	728,169	730,481
(Minus) depreciation expense	(203,091)	(194,528)
Cash paid to suppliers and employees	$4,012,742	$3,897,606

Since operating expenses that are not paid for do not result in cash outflows, an additional adjustment for increases in prepaids and accruals is made if applicable. Note that no such adjustment was necessary for Deere. Finally, interest expense and taxes paid are added to arrive at cash disbursed for operating activities.

A digression seems in order to explain how income taxes paid were calculated. Although income taxes usually require cash payments, tax credits and net changes in the accrued and deferred tax accounts can result in a net cash inflow. The manner in which the accrued and deferred tax accounts are managed can result in a permanent source of cash that, if it did not exist, would have to be replaced by other permanent sources.

This important fact can be illustrated by the tax account for Deere. Even though the company enjoyed a $64,498,000 tax credit in 1985, the combined effect of the tax account resulted in a cash outflow for income taxes of $10,477,000. There are two aspects of the income tax account that may be responsible for this outcome. First, accrued tax expense represents a postponement of paying income tax expense. Second, deferred tax is that portion of income tax expense that does not decrease net cash. The combined effects on Deere's cash flow can be seen below:

1984 Accrued income taxes		$350,322
+ 1985 Income taxes due		(6,949)
1984 Deferred income tax	$108,073	
+ 1985 Income tax expense	(64,498)	
− 1985 Deferred income tax	50,524	
= 1985 Income taxes due	$ (6,949)	
− 1985 Accrued income taxes		332,896
= 1985 Cash outlay (inflow) for income taxes		$ 10,477

Net cash flow from operations is then calculated by subtracting operating cash disbursements from operating cash receipts.

Indirect versus Direct Approach.   The principal advantage of using the indirect approach is that it provides insight into the quality of earnings by focusing on the difference between net income and cash flow from operations. The direct approach, it is argued, is merely a cash-basis income statement that will confuse users accustomed to accrual-based financial statements. Furthermore, proponents of the indirect approach point out that it is cost justified. Since information is maintained on an accrual basis, the indirect approach will not require changes in current accounting practices. In other words, no additional reporting costs are incurred to present the statement of changes in financial position in this manner.

In contrast, proponents of the direct approach argue that by focusing on the major operating cash receipts and payments, this method provides the basic cash flow information related to the operation of a business. It gives the clearest picture of where operating cash came from and how it was spent. For this reason, it is the most helpful approach for analyzing past trends and estimating future cash flows from operations. In addition, the indirect approach can be misleading since it appears that various adjustments to operating income, namely depreciation, depletion, and amortization, are cash inflows.

The use of the indirect approach can also lead to inaccuracies in the calculation of cash flow from operations. When using it, for example, acquisitions and divestitures, the absorption cost method for valuing manufactured inventories, or reclassification of items within the balance sheet can lead to incorrect values. Despite these and other problems, the indirect method still received the support of five of the seven members of the FASB. The two dissenting members stated that "by permitting the continued use of the indirect method, the Board has foregone the opportunity to make a significant contribution to the quality of financial reporting and to enhanced user understanding of cash flows from operating activities."

Net Income versus Cash Flow from Operations.   The accrual-based counterpart of cash flow from operations is net income. A comparison of the two concepts, shown in Table 3-4, is revealing. Note that the basic components of CFFO and net income — sales, cost of sales, and operating expenses — are the same. The difference lies in the adjustments made to generate CFFO: sales are adjusted by the change in accounts receivable, cost of sales are adjusted by the changes in inventories and accounts payable, and operating expenses are adjusted by depreciation expense and changes in accruals and prepaids. Net income for Deere decreased from $104,944 in 1984 to $30,505 in 1985. During that same period, CFFO increased from $248,059 to $337,592.

TABLE 3-4. Comparison of Net Income with Cash Flow from Operations

Operating Profit	*Cash Flow from Operations*
Net sales	Net sales
	− Change in accounts receivable
	− Change in other current assets
	= Cash provided by operating activities
− Cost of sales	− Cost of sales
	− Change in inventory
	+ Change in accounts payable
= Gross profit	
− Operating expenses	− Operating expenses (excluding depreciation)
	+ Change in other current liabilities
	− Change in prepaids
	+ Change in accruals
= Operating profit	
− Interest expense	− Interest expense
= Before-tax profit	
− Income tax	− Income tax
	+ Change in accrued taxes
	+ Change in deferred taxes
Net income	= Cash flow from operations

Sales and cash receipts are not the same when there is a significant variation in accounts receivable. Expenses and cash disbursements are not the same when inventory levels, accounts payable, or accruals fluctuate to any degree. Thus, from a liquidity standpoint net income is not an adequate measure of a firm's short-term ability to generate cash flow from operations.

Cash Flows from Investing Activities.   Certain transactions that are not central to the operation itself are classified as investing activities. These include interest and dividends on securities held (except highly liquid short-term securities such as treasury bills and certificates of deposit) and the purchase and sale of fixed assets. Net cash flow from investing activities is the sum of nonoperating expenses (net of nonoperating revenues) plus any balance sheet account increases for fixed assets, intangibles, and other noncurrent assets.

To comply with the provisions of the cash flow standards required by FASB 95, the effects of each significant investing activity should be reported separately. For example, both the cash outflows for the acquisition of property, plant, and equipment and the cash inflows from their sale should reported. Related transactions should be reported together if they add to the clarity of the presentation. For example, when old equipment is sold and replaced by the purchase of new equipment, it is appropriate to deduct the proceeds from the sale of the old equipment from the cost of the new. Reporting net values in either case, where data for the separate transactions are available, however, is not appropriate.

Incomplete data may present a problem for the outside analyst who does not have access to the more detailed information. Although the method of presentation suggested in Tables 3-2 and 3-3 minimizes the effects of incomplete data, it assumes that detailed information on the sale and acquisition of fixed assets is not available. Thus, the suggested method of presentation records the net change in gross fixed assets and an adjustment to accumulated depreciation as investing activities.

It may be useful to understand the extent of the loss of information when investing activities are reported in this manner. All transactions relating to the change in net fixed assets can be stated as follows:

> Net fixed assets at the beginning of the year
> \+ Additions to fixed assets
> \- Book value of fixed assets sold during the year
> \- (+) Gain (loss) on the sale of gross fixed assets
> \- Depreciation expense for the year
> _____
> = Net fixed assets at the end of the year

This detailed presentation includes the adjustment to accumulated depreciation that takes into consideration the accumulated depreciation eliminated from the balance sheet due to the sale of fixed assets. The adjustment for Deere in 1984 is calculated as follows:

1984 Accumulated depreciation	$1,451,468
− 1984 Depreciation expense	203,091
− 1983 Accumulated depreciation	1,328,018
If $\left\{{> \atop =}\right\}$ 0 then $\left\{{\text{Accumulated depreciation sold} \atop \text{No adjustment}}\right\}$	$ 79,641

A value greater than zero indicates that accumulated depreciation was eliminated from the balance sheet due to the sale of fixed assets. If the above calculation were equal to zero, this would indicate there was no sale of fixed assets during the year and no adjustment necessary. The aggregate cash flows recorded as investing activities are simply the changes in gross fixed assets, the accumulated depreciation adjustment, and the change in other noncurrent assets. In 1984, Deere's investing activities resulted in a net cash flow outflow of $147,514. In the following year, it showed an even larger net cash outflow of $199,355.

Cash Flows from Financing Activities. Cash flows from financing activities measures the amount of funds provided by external financing. It is calculated by netting new borrowings and equities transactions against current-debt service and dividends paid. New borrowings include both short-term notes and long-term debt. Equity transactions include increases in preferred and common stock, additions to paid-in capital, and purchase of treasury stock. Current debt service includes amortization of current maturities of long-term debt and short-term notes payable. New borrowings and equity transactions netted against current debt service and dividends paid results in a cash outflow through financial activities in both years for Deere: $(274,106) and $(91,737) in 1984 and 1985, respectively.

In addition to the normal income statement and balance sheet data, information is needed to determine conclusively values for short-term debt amortization, new borrowing (both short- and long-term), and additional long-term debt amortization. But even without this additional information, reasonable estimates can be made for each of these values.

Short-term notes are by definition obligations that must be paid within 1 year. Thus, it is reasonable to assume that the short-term notes that are recorded on one balance sheet will be paid within the ensuing year and not show up on the next balance sheet. Additionally, any short-term debt obligations recorded on the new balance must have involved transactions that occurred in that year.

A single calculation can be used to estimate the activity in long-term debt. By definition, the value recorded for current maturities of long-term debt is the amount that will be paid within the next year. With no transactions involving long-term debt other than the retirement of current maturities, the sum of current maturities and long-term debt in a given year should equal the value for long-term debt in the previous year. This is enough information to estimate a value for additional long-term debt amortization (ADA) or new long-term borrowing. The calculations for Deere for 1984 and 1985 follow:

	1984	1985
Long-term debt $n - 1$	$1,180,295	$ 972,185
− Long-term debt n	(972,185)	(1,110,087)
− Current maturities n	(157,833)	(16,351)
If $\begin{cases} > \\ = \\ < \end{cases}$ 0 then $\begin{cases} \text{ADA} \\ \text{No activity} \\ \text{New long-term debt} \end{cases}$	$ 50,277	$ (154,253)

Since the value in 1984 is greater than zero, it indicates that there was net additional debt amortization in that year. This is shown as a cash outflow. In 1985 the value is less than zero, indicating net new borrowing and cash inflow. A value equal to zero would indicate no net activity.

An additional adjustment to retained earnings may be necessary if the financial statements from previous years were adjusted in any way or the firm transacted its own stock for a price other than book value. To determine whether such an adjustment is necessary, construct a net worth reconciliation statement as discussed in Chapter 2. If the statement does not balance, an adjustment to cash flow equal to the discrepancy will be required. The format is

1983 Retained earnings	$1,877,448
+ 1984 After-tax earnings	104,944
− 1984 Dividends paid	67,772
− 1984 Retained earnings	1,914,524

$$\text{If} \begin{Bmatrix} > \\ = \\ < \end{Bmatrix} 0 \text{ then } \begin{Bmatrix} \text{Cash required} \\ \text{No adjustment} \\ \text{Cash provided} \end{Bmatrix} \qquad \$ \quad 96$$

Since the calculation results in a value less than zero, an adjustment is required. A zero value would indicate that no adjustment is needed. Amounts greater than zero would indicate cash is required; amounts less than zero indicate cash provided.

A final word of caution on reporting aggregated information is in order. Ideally, each individual investing and financing transaction should be reported separately. Both the purchase and sale of unrelated fixed assets should be shown. Retirement of debt and new borrowings should be reported separately rather than netted against one another. Although this is not always possible for the outside analyst, the suggested format minimizes the amount of built-in aggregation. Thus, when separate information is available, report it separately.

Change in Cash Balance. The change in cash balance (cash and cash equivalents) is calculated by summing the cash flows from operating, investing, and financing. The net change in cash is equal to cash flow from operations minus cash flow used in investing activities (plus cash flow provided) plus the cash flow provided by financing activities (minus cash flow used). This value is the actual change in the cash and cash equivalents accounts on the balance sheet between any two consecutive years. Cash balances at Deere decreased by $173,561 in 1984 and increased by $45,600 in 1985.

REPORTING NONCASH TRANSACTIONS

FASB 95 requires that certain types of noncash transactions must be reported on the cash flow statement. Even though the transactions do not involve the transfer of cash, they are significant because of their potential impact on future cash flows. The transactions include debt-to-equity conversions, asset acquisitions completed by the assumption of liabilities (including capitalized lease obligations), and all other exchanges of assets or liabilities.

Future users of cash flow statements will see noncash transactions presented in one of two ways. They may either be reported in the statement of cash flows itself or in a separate schedule. The only requirement is that the manner of presentation clearly identify that the transactions do not involve the receipt or payment of cash.

Financial statements generated before 1987 will create some analytical problems for outside analysts and researchers. In most cases, it will be difficult to distinguish the extent of these types of transactions. The use of income statement and balance sheet information will allow the user to distinguish only aggregate flows. Conversions of debt to equity will be seen as additional long-term debt amortization and increases in equity. Although the aggregate numbers are correct, they can imply cash inflows and outflows where none in fact occurred. In effect, the cash flow statement generated from income statement and balance sheet information alone will present aggregate data without the required separate schedule of noncash transactions.

A simple example can show the potential information loss of the aggregate presentation. The cash flow statement for Diadelosa, Inc., is given in Table 3-5. In addition to the obvious activity shown on the statement, suppose the following transactions took place during the year:

1. The purchase of $8,000 in property, plant, and equipment was completed with a $2,000 cash payment, a $5,000 long-term mortgage, and a $1,000 capital lease.
2. The cash sale of $2,000 in property, plant, and equipment for book value was completed.
3. The assets of Simmons Company were acquired. A cash payment of $1,000, a long-term note of $1,000, and the assumption of $1,000 in long-term debt secured the $3,000 in assets.
4. Common stock of $250 was issued to settle $250 in long-term debt.

TABLE 3-5. Diadelosa's Cash Flow Statement

Cash Flows from Operating Activities	
Net Cash Flow from Operations	$2,100
Cash Flows from Investing Activities	
Increase in gross fixed assets	$5,000
Increase in other noncurrent assets	2,000
Cash Flow Requirements from Investing Activities	$7,000
Cash Flows from Financing Activities	
New long-term borrowing	$5,000
Minus debt amortization	
Short-term notes	100
Current maturities of long-term debt	150
Additional debt amortization	250
Plus increase in common stock	250
Minus dividends paid	100
Cash Flow Provided from Financing Activities	$4,350
Change in Cash Balance	$ (250)
Schedule of Investing and Financing Activities Not Shown	
Acquisition of Gross Fixed Assets	
Fixed assets acquired	$8,000
Fixed assets sold	(2,000)
Capital lease incurred	(1,000)
Change in gross fixed assets	$5,000
Acquisition of Simmons Company	
Noncurrent assets acquired	$3,000
Long-term debt assumed	(1,000)
Change in noncurrent assets	$2,000
Common stock issued to settle long-term debt	$ 250

The aggregate effects of the first two transactions are seen in the increase in gross fixed assets of $5,000 and the new long-term debt of $5,000. The third transaction is shown as a $2,000 increase in other noncurrent assets. The fourth is shown as an additional debt amortization of $250 and an increase in common stock of $250. Without the additional information given above, the information in this paragraph is all that would be known about the activity. The complete cash flow statement will include a schedule such as the one in Table 3-5, clearly identifying the noncash transactions that took place during the year.

The loss of information due to aggregation is not fatal to the analysis. It is, however, important that users of cash flow statements be aware of the common noncash investing and financing activities and understand the limited information content of aggregate data.

CASH FLOW EFFECTS OF FOREIGN EXCHANGE RATES

Whenever financial statements are translated from the currency of one country to that of another, certain adjustments are necessary because of changes in foreign exchange rates during the reporting period. In the case in which the foreign subsidiary of a firm (e.g., located in the United Kingdom) conducts its operations in the local currency (British pounds), financial reporting must translate those statements into the reporting currency of the consolidated entity (dollars in the case of a U.S.-based corporation).

There is more to translating financial statements from one currency to another than adjusting account balances by changes in the foreign exchange rate. To translate a cash flow statement from one currency to another requires the firm to develop a separate local currency cash flow statement for each foreign subsidiary and to translate the local currency cash flow statements into the reporting currency using the exchange rate in effect at the time of the cash flows. If the second step is impractical, a weighted average exchange rate may be used.

Since the purpose of the cash flow statement is to report cash inflows and cash outflows during an operating period, the suggested approach seems appropriate. The drawback to the approach is that the cash flow statement translated in this manner cannot be used to reconcile two successive balance sheets. The reason is twofold: Cash and equivalents are translated at exchange rates that exist at the ends of each of the respective years, and changes in other balance sheet accounts are translated at foreign exchange rates that exist at the time of the cash flows or more often by use of a weighted average.

To illustrate the impact of the reporting requirement for the cash flow statement, assume the comparative balance sheet presented in Table 3-6 for InterCorp, a U.K. subsidiary of a U.S. corporation that uses the British pound (£).

The exchange rates from British pounds to U.S. dollars were 1.4445 and 1.4745 on December 31, 1985, and 1986, respectively. The appropriately weighted average exchange rate for 1986 was 1.4670. Assume the only change in gross fixed assets was a £3 million purchase of equipment at the beginning of 1986. Dividends of £10 million were paid at the end of 1986. All other transactions were distributed evenly throughout the year.

The cash flow statement for InterCorp using the indirect approach is given in Table 3-7 (in both pounds and dollars).

The dollar change in cash balances is calculated as follows: (£28,500 × 1.4745) − (£23,600 × 1.4445). The translated cash flow

TABLE 3-6. InterCorp's Comparative Balance Sheet

Thousands of Pounds	1985	1986
Assets		
Cash and equivalents	£ 23,600	£ 28,500
Accounts receivable	12,500	13,800
Inventory	31,600	48,400
Prepaids	1,500	2,500
Total Current Assets	£ 69,200	£ 93,200
Gross fixed assets	121,000	124,000
Accumulated depreciation	(48,400)	(60,800)
Total Assets	£141,800	£156,400
Liabilities and Equity		
Accounts payable	£ 32,500	£ 25,800
Accruals	2,600	4,500
Short-term notes	10,000	14,400
Total Current Assets	£ 45,100	£ 44,700
Common stock	25,000	25,000
Retained earnings	25,300	45,200
Total Liabilities and Equity	£141,800	£156,400

TABLE 3-7. InterCorp Translated Cash Flow Statement

(000s)	Pounds	Exchange Rate	Dollars
Operating activities:			
Net Income	£ 29,900	1.4670	$ 43,863
Noncash items:			
+ Depreciation	12,400	1.4670	18,191
− Increase in Receivables	(1,300)	1.4670	(1,907)
− Increase in Inventory	(16,800)	1.4670	(24,646)
− Increase in Prepaids	(1,000)	1.4670	(1,467)
− Decrease in Payables	(6,700)	1.4670	(9,829)
+ Increase in Accruals	1,900	1.4670	2,787
− Decrease in Deferred	(1,400)	1.4670	(2,054)
Net Cash Flow from Operating Activities	£ 17,000		$ 24,938
Investing activities:			
Increase in Fixed Assets	£(3,000)	1.4445	$ (4,334)
Cash Flow Requirements From Investing	£(3,000)		$ (4,334)
Financing activities:			
+ New Short-Term Notes	£ 4,400	1.4670	$ 6,455
− Repayment of LTD	(3,500)	1.4670	(5,135)
− Dividends Paid	(10,000)	1.4745	(14,745)
Cash Flow Requirements from Financing	£(9,100)		$(13,425)
Exchange rate effect	NA		$ 753
Change in Cash Balances	£ 4,900		$ 7,932

statement must reconcile to this change after the translation from the functional to the reporting currency. This requirement may be fulfilled by reporting the effect of the exchange rate change on cash as a separate line item. As such, it is not an operating, investing, or financing activity. But it is reported as part of the reconciliation in cash balances during the accounting period. Although it is viewed as a plug figure, the effect of the exchange rate change may be calculated as follows:

Cash at the beginning of the year	£23,600	
× Change in exchange rate (1.4745 − 1.4445)	× 0.03	
= Exchange rate effect on beginning cash		$708.0
Cash flow from operations	£24,200	
+ Cash flow from short-term borrowing	4,400	
= Total cash receipts	£28,600	
× Change in exchange rate (1.4745 − 1.4670)	×0.0075	
= Exchange rate effect on cash receipts		+$214.5
Increase in gross fixed assets	£ 3,000	
× Change in exchange rate (1.4745 − 1.4445)	× 0.03	
= Exchange rate effect on gross fixed assets		−$ 90.0
Repayment of long-term debt	£ 3,500	
× Change in exchange rate (1.4745 − 1.4760)	×0.0075	
= Exchange rate effect on repayment of debt		−$ 80.25
Effect of exchange rate changes on cash		$752.25

CASH FLOW ANALYSIS

A clear cash flow presentation enhances the understanding of the financial position of a business entity. Cash flow analysis can contribute to a complete financial analysis by enabling the analyst to project future cash flows, assess the quality of a firm's income, evaluate the ability of a firm to maintain a certain level of operations, and determine a firm's financial flexibility and liquidity.

Project Future Cash Flows

Accurate financial reporting has always been a top priority of the FASB. In "Concepts Statement No. 1" (FASB, 1983), the FASB states that one of the primary objectives of financial statement reporting is to improve the ability of users to predict the amount, timing, and certainty of future cash flows. Cash flow data presented in the activity format, along with profitability data from the income statement, provide the necessary information to enable users to predict future flows.

Assess the Quality of Income

Whether cash flow is more reliable than net income in determining the financial condition of a firm is the subject of considerable debate. It is certain, however, that financial obligations must be paid in cash. Working capital or net income is not an acceptable part of the settlement of a debt. The use of both cash flow and income statement data provides information on the ability of a firm to turn income into cash. The higher the ratio of cash flow to net income, the more reliable the profitability measures as indicators of performance.

This discussion is not meant to imply that cash flow from operations, or one of its components, is a superior indicator of financial performance, only that it provides valuable information in assessing the quality of net income. The FASB, recognizing the confusion that would inevitably result over this issue, determined that cash flow should not be reported on a per share basis.

The major analytical problems in reporting earnings per share data have been debated widely in the financial accounting literature and are largely settled. But the same cannot be said with respect to reporting cash flow per share. At this stage in the development of the cash flow concept, it would be confusing to users of financial statements to see cash flow per share reported. If cash flow from operations were reported on a per share basis, it would imply that these funds were available for distribution in the form of dividends whereas, in fact, most of these funds may be required to repay debt and reinvest in plant and equipment.

Eventually, the issue of cash flow per share reporting will be resolved in the literature. Until such time, cash flow per share reporting might needlessly mislead and confuse financial statement users.

Evaluate the Ability to Maintain Operations

If a firm is to continue as a viable entity, it must be able to fulfill its current obligations, service its debt (both principal and interest), and provide its owners with a reasonable return on their investment. To accomplish this successfully and provide for future growth (essential for the development of a secondary equity market), the firm must be able to generate adequate cash flow from operations. Cash flow analysis is the only means of determining whether the firm is providing cash from operations or whether it has prospects of doing so in the future.

Determine Financial Flexibility and Liquidity

Cash flow information is essential in determining the financial flexibility and liquidity position of a business operation. Financial flexibility is the ability of a firm to take advantage of unexpected opportunities or respond to unexpected requirements by changing the amount or timing of cash flows. Financial flexibility depends on the stability of a firm's earnings, affecting its ability to generate funds internally, the debt-to-equity position of the firm, affecting its access to external financing, and the availability of lines of credit.

Liquidity is the opportunity cost (time and money) of converting assets into cash. Information on cash flows will help identify potential problems that a firm may have in fulfilling current obligations as they come due or altering the timing of asset conversions into cash. As shown in Chapter 4, liquidity is determined by a firm's dependence on external financing. The greater the reliance on external financing, the less liquid the operation.

SUMMARY

The cash flow statement provides information that is unavailable from the income statement and the balance sheet. By specifically categorizing activities as operating, investing, and financing, it helps users answer questions about future cash flows that cannot be answered with traditional accrual-based methods. The format of the cash flow statement used in this chapter conforms to the guidelines established by the FASB. The basic components are the same as those in the statement of changes in financial position using a cash definition of funds. But instead of being organized according to sources and uses, cash flows are categorized according to type of activity—operating, investing, and financing—allowing liquidity problems to be isolated more readily.

Cash flow analysis focuses on financial flexibility and liquidity, concepts that are not adequately measured by traditional ratio techniques. In today's business and financial environment, it is increasingly important to pay close attention to these measures of a company's financial health and performance.

REFERENCES

Financial Accounting Standards Board. 1983. *Accounting Standards: Statement of Financial Accounting Concepts 1–4*. New York: McGraw-Hill Book Company.

Financial Accounting Series. November 1987. Statement of cash flows. *Statement of Financial Accounting Standards No. 95*. Stamford, CT: Financial Accounting Standards Board.

Drtina, Ralph E., and James A. Largay III. 1985. Pitfalls in calculating cash flow from operations. *The Accounting Review* 60(2):314–326.

Gombola, Michael J., and J. Edward Ketz. 1981. Alternative measures of cash flow—Part two. *Cashflow* 2(1):39–42.

Maness, Terry S., and James W. Henderson. 1985. Check the corporate pulse by administering cash flow analysis. *Cashflow* 6(4):38–40.

Seed, Allen H. III. 1984. The funds statement: How can it be improved?: *Financial Executive* 52(10):52–55.

Chapter 4

Analyzing Cash Flow from Operations

The primary concern of a complete cash flow analysis is to determine the causes of a particular level of cash flow and ascertain why changes in that level have occurred. For example, an increase in cash flow from operations may result from instituting stringent credit policies, maintaining lower levels of inventory, stretching payables, and/or delaying payments to employees. Although these measures will increase cash flow in the short run, they can result in customer and creditor reactions that may actually reduce cash flow in the long run.

In approximately half of the financially distressed firms studied by Viscione (1985), the positive cash flows from operations were the result of significant decreases in accounts receivable and inventory or significant increases in accounts payable and accrued expenses. In these cases, changes in the current asset and current liability categories were as responsible as current sales for the positive cash flow values observed. Viscione's results highlight the importance of interpreting cash flow measures within the context of an integrated financial framework.

Whereas it is important to recognize significant trends in cash flow from operations, it is also important to know and understand the causes of the observed changes. If the accounts receivable balance is trending downward, it is important to know the reasons for the decline. Is it because the current level of sales is trending downward, or because credit policies are changing? Or are customer payment patterns changing? Liquidity analysis depends on finding answers to these types of questions. Separate cash flow analysis is not enough. An integrative approach using both cash flow and traditional analysis is essential.

The first step in developing an integrative approach is a thorough understanding of the analytical framework for studying cash flows from operating activities. The following sections present a framework for examining the liquidity of a firm based on its operating activities. Several approaches to the analysis of this important barometer of financial health, namely, cash flow from operations, are developed and discussed. Chapter 5 will then present a more comprehensive view of liquidity by incorporating the analysis of financial flexibility, that is, the cash flows that result from the investing and financing activities of the business enterprise.

IMPORTANCE OF CASH FLOW FROM OPERATIONS

Until recently net profit or net profit plus depreciation of a firm was seen as reasonable proxies for cash flow. More than any other event, the bankruptcy of W.T. Grant in the mid-1970s led to a change in that perspective. Case studies of the W.T. Grant bankruptcy have prompted analysts and researchers to focus on developing a better understanding of the usefulness of cash flow and of the relationship between cash flow and profitability measures.

In one of the most frequently cited articles dealing with cash flow analysis, Largay and Stickney (1980) examined the benefits of tracking cash flow from operations. The results of their study indicate that a careful monitoring of the cash flow of W.T. Grant would have provided an early warning signal of its ultimate bankruptcy and subsequent liquidation.

Based on published information, it is clear that W.T. Grant's operations had been a net user of cash for 8 out of the 10 operating years before the company went bankrupt in 1975.[1] This result seems to indicate that tracking the cash flow from operations would provide an early warning signal of potential liquidity problems.

Largay and Stickney's observations served to encourage later work in two related areas. First, research was conducted that statistically compared various measures of profitability and cash flow. Second, several

---

[1] For purposes of their study, cash flow from operations was defined as follows:

> Net Income
> + Noncash Charges
> − Change in Accounts Receivable and Inventory
> + Change in Accounts Payable and Accruals
>
> = Cash Flow From Operations

bankruptcy prediction studies were undertaken to determine whether including cash flow variables in bankruptcy models improved the predictive capabilities of those models. Results of these bankruptcy studies will be discussed in Chapter 7.

RELATIONSHIP BETWEEN PROFIT AND CASH FLOW

The fact that the more traditional ratios, including profitability ratios and turnover ratios, did not provide the early warning signals in the W.T. Grant case concerned and perplexed many financial managers. This prompted a series of inquiries into the relationships among the profitability and cash flow measures.

Gombola and Ketz (1981a, 1981b) reported the results of a statistical comparison of various profitability and cash flow measures. The study proved to be important because, at the time, the term cash flow did not have a standard definition for calculation purposes. They tested the relationships among four measures — net income, net income plus depreciation, working capital from operations, and cash flow from operations.

In general, their study concluded that it is improper to assume that the various measures disclose the same information concerning the operation. The concepts, although related, are not identical. More specifically, they determined the following: (1) Net income is not a good substitute for cash flow since some accruals and deferrals are significant. (2) Net income plus depreciation is not a good proxy for cash flow from operations even though historically this is the most commonly used measure for cash flow. (3) The significance of long-term accruals causes net income plus depreciation to be a poor substitute for working capital from operations. (4) Short-term accruals were significant, resulting in somewhat different values for working capital from operations and cash flow from operations. Their conclusions indicated that cash flow from operations is a unique measure of cash flow, containing information that is not available in the other three measures.

EARLY ATTEMPTS AT ANALYZING THE OPERATING CASH CYCLE

Liquidity in the form of the current assets of a firm is continuously moving from one current asset category to another. This must be the case if the firm's current assets are truly liquid. Funds, for example, are originally invested in inventory. After a period of time, the inventory is sold, and either cash or accounts receivable is incremented. If the sale is a cash sale, the transaction is reflected in an increase in the firm's cash balances. A credit sale results in an increase in the accounts receivable balance. The eventual collection of accounts receivable results in an increase in the firm's cash balances. During this cycle, various payments are made to workers and suppliers. Funds owed to these groups are reflected in accounts payable and accruals. As funds become owed these accounts increase, and as payments are made these accounts decrease.

There have been many attempts at developing tools for analyzing the component parts of the operating cycle and even the entire cycle. Harold Bierman (1960), for example, developed two ratios designed to address the number of days of liquidity stored in the net working capital balances. His approach was to create two specific ratios that would relate a flow variable to net working capital, one for firms with a positive net working capital position and another for those with a negative net working capital position. His flow variable was cash flow, defined as net income plus noncash charges; that is, depletion, depreciation, and amortization.

For those firms experiencing a negative net working capital position, the basic liquidity measure is

$$\frac{\text{Current Liabilities} - \text{Current Assets}}{\text{Net Income} + \text{Noncash Charges}} \times 365$$

This ratio gives the required number of days of cash flow to cover current liabilities net of current or liquid assets. Liquid assets may be substituted for current assets.

For firms with a positive net working capital position that are experiencing a deficit cash flow from operations, the ratio needs to be modified; Bierman suggests the following:

$$\frac{\text{Current Assets} - \text{Current Liabilities}}{\text{Funds Lost in Operations}} \times 365$$

This form of liquidity ratio provides the number of days supply of net current assets.

In developing these ratios, Bierman attempted to integrate information from the funds statement with the traditional liquidity ratios to provide a more comprehensive analysis. Even though these ratios offer an improvement over the traditional static measures of liquidity (e.g., the current ratio), even Bierman admits that they are not applicable to all situations and in fact are meaningless under certain circumstances.

Using a different approach, Sorter and Benston (1960) provide additional insight into the integration of the traditional static liquidity measures and funds flow information. They suggested a framework for studying liquidity that they called *interval analysis*. They considered that all firms have certain defensive assets, such as cash, marketable securities, and receivables. Projected daily expenditures were approximated by taking the direct and indirect costs from the current income statement and then adjusting for noncash expenses and known future changes in operations. They then expressed this liquidity measure as the number of days a company could survive under the specified conditions.

Studies have shown that a firm's ranking on a liquidity scale according to a defensive interval measure is substantially different from its ranking from the current ratio. Examples of interval measures suggested by Sorter and Benston are as follows:

$$\text{Basic Defensive Interval} = \frac{\text{Defensive Assets}}{\text{Projected Daily Cash Expenditure}}$$

$$\text{No Credit Interval} = \frac{\text{Defensive Assets} - \text{Actual Liabilities}}{\text{Projected Daily Cash Expenditure}}$$

$$\text{Cash Interval} = \frac{\text{Cash} + \text{Marketable Securities}}{\text{Projected Daily Cash Expenditure}}$$

$$\text{Reduced Sales Interval} = \frac{\text{Defensive Assets}}{\text{Projected Daily Expenditures} - \text{Projected Daily Receipts}}$$

One weakness of this analysis is that it does not actually focus on the process that firms use to pay their debts. Sales revenues or, more specifically, cash receipts generated from operations are the normal way bills and debts are paid. Thus, the static concept of defensive assets should be replaced with the more dynamic and realistic concept of cash flow.

Fraser (1983) developed a liquidity index by combining cash assets (cash plus marketable securities) and cash flow from operations and dividing the result by current liabilities. If this ratio is increasing over time, it signals an increasing level of liquidity. If it is declining, it signals potential liquidity problems. Fraser's liquidity ratio (FLR) is defined as follows:

$$\text{FLR} = \frac{\text{CFFO}_t + \text{CA}_t}{\text{CL}_t}$$

where

CFFO_t = Cash flow from operations in period t

CA_t = Cash assets (cash plus marketable securities) at the end of period t

CL_t = Current liabilities at the end of period t

The use of the Fraser liquidity ratio as a measure of liquidity can be justified as follows. The first term in the numerator represents a firm's ability to generate cash internally out of operations. In other words, $CFFO_t$ is the addition to the stock of cash assets originating from within the operation itself during the accounting period. The second term represents liquid current assets; that is, CA_t is the stock of cash available at the outset of any accounting period. The denominator, CL_t, represents obligations (cash outflows) that come due during the accounting period.

In general, the measure is a valid index of the liquidity position of a firm. The problem with Fraser's approach is the way the ratio is calculated. More specifically, the use of end-of-period values for cash assets and current liabilities and intraperiod cash flow from operations is a mixing of time periods, introducing a significant bias in the measure.

According to Fraser, CFFO can be "viewed as a substitute for inventory and accounts receivable in the existing current ratio, and as a proxy for the ability of the firm to translate inventory and accounts receivable into cash." Considering that it is beginning inventory (I_{t-1}) and accounts receivable (AR_{t-1}) that are being translated into cash, $CFFO_t$ is a proxy for I_{t-1} and AR_{t-1}. In this regard, it makes as much intuitive sense to match CA_t with $CFFO_t$ in the numerator as it would to match it with I_{t-1} and AR_{t-1}.

In addition, Fraser indicated that "adding CFFO to cash assets would appear to be double-counting." And indeed the double-counting of cash flows can be clearly shown.[2] Since the end-of-period cash assets have already been incremented by the cash flow from operations, it is counted twice in the numerator. This, however, may not be the most serious aspect of the index's bias. As the proof clearly shows, Fraser's liquidity ratio includes two other cash flow categories — cash flow from investing and cash flow from financing — in addition to double-counting cash flow from operations.

Cash flow from investing is positive when assets are sold and negative when they are purchased. Cash flow from financing is positive when new long-term sources such as loans, bonds, and equity are obtained and negative when financial obligations are retired. Thus, the Fraser liquidity ratio could increase even when cash flow from operations is negative if assets are sold and/or new sources of long-term financing are obtained. If a user of the Fraser liquidity ratio is unaware of the inclusion of these additional cash flows, changes in the value of the index may be misinterpreted.

Finally, when using Fraser's ratio, analysts are implicitly assuming that investment and financing activities will combine to provide the same amount of cash in the projection period as they did historically. It seems reasonable to question the validity of this assumption.

Clearly, the ratio intends to measure cash inflows and compare them with cash outflows. Therefore, cash inflows should be defined as the sum of the cash assets of a firm at the beginning of an accounting period plus what the firm is able to generate from operations in that same period. Likewise, the current cash outflows should be defined as the obligations of a firm that will come due within that accounting period (beginning current liabilities).

By necessity the ratio must be redefined to eliminate the biases discussed above. The ratio is restated below and referred to as the current liquidity ratio (CLR):

$$\mathrm{CLR} = \frac{\mathrm{CA}_{t-1} + \mathrm{CFFO}_t}{\mathrm{CL}_{t-1}}$$

Given these adjustments, the ratio is an easily calculated measure of liquidity that can be used by outside analysts and investors as well as analysts associated with a firm.

---

[2] First, define end-of-period cash assets (CA_t) as being equal to beginning-of-period cash assets (CA_{t-1}) plus the change in cash assets during the period ($\Delta\mathrm{CA}$):

$$\mathrm{CA}_t = \mathrm{CA}_{t-1} + \Delta\mathrm{CA}$$

Next, define the change in cash assets during the period as the sum of cash flow from operating activities in period t (CFFO_t), cash flow from investing activities in period t (CFFI_t), and cash flow from financing activities in period t (CFFF_t):

$$\Delta\mathrm{CA} = \mathrm{CFFO}_t + \mathrm{CFFI}_t + \mathrm{CFFF}_t$$

By substitution, the numerator in the current liquidity ratio as presented by Fraser can be redefined as follows:

$$
\begin{aligned}
\mathrm{CA}_t + \mathrm{CFFO}_t &= \mathrm{CA}_{t-1} + \Delta\mathrm{CA} + \mathrm{CFFO}_t \\
&= \mathrm{CA}_{t-1} + \mathrm{CFFO}_t + \mathrm{CFFI}_t + \mathrm{CFFF}_t + \mathrm{CFFO}_t \\
&= \mathrm{CA}_{t-1} + 2\,\mathrm{CFFO}_t + \mathrm{CFFI}_t + \mathrm{CFFF}_t
\end{aligned}
$$

RECENT DEVELOPMENTS IN CASH CYCLE ANALYSIS

Recently, the analysis of liquidity has focused on using the traditional accrual-based liquidity measures in a slightly different manner. Richards and Laughlin (1980) suggested a useful framework, called the *cash conversion period*, for analyzing the operating cash cycle. Their approach, which measures liquidity from the perspective of a going concern, is contrasted with the traditional liquidation value approach that uses the standard accrual-based liquidity measures. It actually blends operating balance sheet accounts with the various income statement items at a firm's given level of operations.

Calculation of the cash conversion period relies on three accrual-based measures of activity that focus on the working capital cycle of the firm. The first step is to estimate the efficiency of the credit and collections aspect of an operation by calculating the average collection period or DSO. This ratio is a measure of the average number of days it takes for customers to pay for merchandise. DSO is calculated by dividing 365 by the ratio of sales to receivables. Alternatively, it can be derived by dividing the dollar amount of end-of-period receivables on the balance sheet by average daily sales. The DSO calculation for Deere for 1985 is as follows:

$$\text{Days Sales Outstanding} = \frac{365}{\text{Sales/Receivables}}$$

$$\frac{365}{\$4,061/\$2,894} = 261 \text{ days}$$

The next step is to estimate the efficiency of inventory management as measured by the average length of time that an inventory item is in stock before it is sold. This is the days inventory discussed earlier. Conceptually, the ratio measures the number of days between the receipt of an item until it is actually sold to a customer, or the average number of days that inventory sits idle. It is calculated by dividing 365 by the ratio of cost of sales to inventory. Alternatively, the same value can be derived by dividing the end-of-period inventory by the average cost of sales per day. The value for days inventory for Deere is

$$\text{Days Inventory} = \frac{365}{\text{Cost of Sales/Inventory}}$$

$$= \frac{365}{\$3,355/\$447} = 49 \text{ days}$$

The third component in the analysis is an estimate of the efficiency of the accounts payable management as measured by days payable. This ratio is calculated by dividing 365 by the ratio of cost of sales to payables. Alternatively, it may be calculated by dividing the end-of-period accounts payable and accruals by the average daily operating costs, which include cost of goods sold and selling and administrative expenses exclusive of noncash charges. Days payable for Deere is

$$\text{Days Payable} = \frac{365}{\text{Cost of Sales/Payables}}$$

$$= \frac{365}{\$3,355/\$1,027} = 112 \text{ days}$$

The cash conversion period is calculated by adding days sales outstanding to days inventory (a concept referred to as the operating cycle) and then subtracting days payable. For Deere, the cash conversion period in 1985 was 198 days:

Operating Cycle = Days Sales Outstanding + Days Inventory
= 261 days + 49 days
= 310 days

Cash Conversion Period = Operating Cycle − Days Payables
= 310 days − 112 days
= 198 days

Analysts must be careful in interpreting changes in the length of the cash cycle. The cash cycle can be reduced, for example, even if the operating cycle expands by stretching payables by a greater number of days than the operating cycle expands. This is clearly not a signal of increased liquidity. Thus, any changes in the length of the cash cycle must be analyzed according to its cause.

A diagram of the cash conversion period is shown in Figure 4-1. A horizontal time line is used to depict the length of the operating cycle — the time from when inventories are received and final payment for items sold is received. Days payable is the time between the day inventories are received and the day payments are made for those inventories. Days inventory is the time between the receipt of inventories and the sale of final goods. Finally, days sales outstanding is the time between the date of sale and the date of receipt of payment.

The cash conversion period is a measure of the time between a firm's payment for inventories and its customers' payment for finished products. This concept provides useful information for managers who are

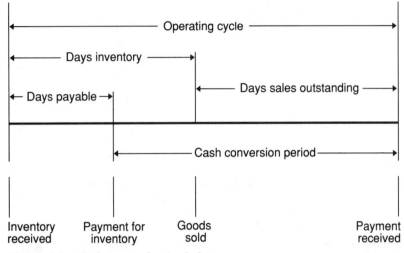

Figure 4-1. Cash conversion period.

responsible for managing and forecasting cash requirements. In practice, it becomes a measure of the time interval over which the financial manager must arrange for nonspontaneous financing. The greater the cash conversion period, the greater the financial strain and the less liquid the firm. A long cash conversion period can absorb a significant amount of liquidity during a period of growing sales and therefore must be managed very carefully.

Quicker turnover of the various current asset accounts, including accounts receivable and inventory, tends to indicate increased efficiency and enhanced cash flow. The analyst must determine the reason for the increased asset turnover to determine whether efficiency has changed or whether management policies have changed. Slower turnover in the liability accounts, including accounts payable and accruals, will also improve the cash cycle. Again, the analyst must make sure that the slower turnover is not affecting relations with suppliers and employees.

ANALYSIS OF THE CASH CONVERSION PERIOD

Proper interpretation of the cash conversion period depends on understanding the cause for changes in its parts. This section explores possible biases in calculating one of the key components of the cash conversion period, namely, days sales outstanding.

Tracking Payment Patterns

A key aspect of cash cycle analysis is monitoring customer payment patterns, that is, determining how fast accounts receivable are converted into cash. The problem facing managers responsible for this task is that the accrual-based measures used to estimate the efficiency of the receivables collection process are not very accurate. They do not adequately address the issue of the timing of inflows and outflows.

The two most popular accrual-based measures are DSO and aging of accounts receivable. But using either of these monitoring devices can result in seriously flawed estimates. The source of the bias is in the calculation of the measures; each depends on two factors unrelated to a firm's collection experience—the recent trend in sales and the sales averaging period used in the calculation.

DSO Bias

As an illustration of the bias in the calculation of days sales outstanding, refer to Table 4-1, which presents the case of the hypothetical firm XYZ Corporation. The firm has a stable collection experience over a period of time in which sales volume varies considerably.

Over the 15-month period shown, average monthly sales steadily increased from quarter to quarter; that is, they went from $150,000 in the first quarter to $350,000 in the last quarter. In the first quarter of the full calendar year (January through March), monthly sales were level. In the subsequent quarters sales rose each month (April through June), then fell each month (July through September), and finally rose and fell (October through December).

Assume that sales are collected according to the following pattern: 20 percent of sales in month one are collected in month one, 50 percent are collected in month two, 20 percent are collected in month three, and 10 percent are collected in month four. In the example, there are no uncollectible accounts.

This particular payment pattern implies an accounts receivable pattern of 80 percent, 30 percent, and 10 percent. That is, 80 percent of

TABLE 4-1. XYZ Corporation's Monthly Sales (thousands of dollars)

October	$100	January	$200	April	$150	July	$400	October	$250
November	250	February	200	May	250	August	300	November	550
December	100	March	200	June	350	September	200	December	250
Average	$150		$200		$250		$300		$350

sales for a given month remain as a receivable balance at the end of the month of sale, 30 percent remain as a balance at the end of the first month, and 10 percent remain as a receivable balance 2 months after the sale. For every $100 in sales each month, $20 is collected in the same month, leaving $80 in accounts receivable at the end of the month. During the month after the sale, $50 will be collected, leaving $30 in the accounts receivable balance. Twenty dollars will be collected in month three, leaving $10 in receivables to be collected in month four.

This fixed rate of customer collections will result in the end-of-month (EOM) accounts receivable balances given in Table 4-2. The values are calculated by following formula:

$$
\begin{array}{l}
80 \text{ Percent of Sales in Month } t \\
+\ 30 \text{ Percent of Sales in Month } t-1 \\
+\ 10 \text{ Percent of Sales in Month } t-2 \\
\hline
=\ \text{Accounts Receivable at End of Month } t
\end{array}
$$

Given these values for sales and end-of-month receivables, the DSO can be calculated. The resulting DSO estimates are shown in Table 4-3 for sales averaging periods of 30, 60, and 90 days, where DSO = Sales averaging period/Sales-to-receivables.

Despite the constant payment pattern assumed in the example, the calculated values for DSO vary considerably. Only in the first quarter

TABLE 4-2. XYZ Corporation's End-of-Month Accounts Receivable (in thousands of dollars)

Month	EOM AR
January	$215
February	230
March	240
April	200
May	265
June	370
July	450
August	395
September	290
October	290
November	535
December	390

TABLE 4-3. XYZ Corporation's Days Sales Outstanding

Quarter Ending	Sales Averaging Periods		
	30 Days	60 Days	90 Days
March 31	$\dfrac{30}{200/240} = 36.0$	$\dfrac{60}{400/240} = 36.0$	$\dfrac{90}{600/240} = 36.0$
June 30	$\dfrac{30}{350/370} = 31.7$	$\dfrac{60}{600/370} = 37.0$	$\dfrac{90}{750/370} = 44.4$
September 30	$\dfrac{30}{200/290} = 43.5$	$\dfrac{60}{500/290} = 34.8$	$\dfrac{90}{900/290} = 29.0$
December 31	$\dfrac{30}{250/390} = 46.8$	$\dfrac{60}{800/390} = 29.3$	$\dfrac{90}{1050/390} = 33.4$

when sales are constant is the DSO calculation the same for each sales averaging period. When sales are rising as in the second quarter, the longer the sales averaging period, the greater the DSO estimate. The opposite is true in the third quarter when sales are declining. A general rule may be derived from this observation: When sales are rising, the shorter the sales averaging period, the lower the DSO estimate; when sales are declining, the longer the sales averaging period, the lower the DSO estimate.

It would be difficult to say that one sales averaging period provides more accurate estimates of DSO than any other. In the example, the 60-day averaging period provides estimates that vary less than either the 30- or 90-day periods. This, however, is not a good generalization and will vary from case to case.

Accounts Receivable Aging Bias

Another popular way to track accounts receivable collections is through the *accounts receivable aging schedule*. Again, the relevant issue is whether the information provided by the schedule accurately reflects the collection experience of the firm.

Using the same sales and customer payment pattern, the accounts receivable balance at the end of each month is provided in Table 4-4. The accounts receivable balance for each month is calculated by summing the figures in each column. For example, the accounts receivable balance at the end of the first quarter (i.e., end of March) is $240,000. Based on the previous discussion, 10 percent of January's sales, 30 percent of February's sales, and 80 percent of March's sales are outstand-

TABLE 4-4. XYZ Corporation's Accounts Receivable Balance Matrix (in thousands of dollars)

Month	January	February	March	April	May	June	July	August	September	October	November	December
									End-of-Month Balances			
November	25											
December	30	10										
January	160	60	20									
February		160	60	20								
March			160	60	20							
April				120	45	15						
May					200	75	25					
June						280	105	35				
July							320	120	40			
August								240	90	30		
September									160	60	20	
October										200	75	25
November											440	165
December												200
Total	*215*	*230*	*240*	*200*	*265*	*370*	*450*	*395*	*290*	*290*	*535*	*390*

ing. Each row shows the accounts receivable balance related to a particular month's sales at the end of each succeeding month. For example, Table 4-1 shows that January sales are $200,000. According to Table 4-4, at the end of January $160,000 remains uncollected. At the end of February $60,000 remains uncollected. Finally, at the end of March $20,000 remains uncollected.

The information in Table 4-4 is usually presented in a slightly different format, referred to as the accounts receivable aging schedule. The familiar format for the schedule is presented in Table 4-5. Each entry shows the percentage of the outstanding accounts receivable that are 1, 2, and 3 months old. For example, of the outstanding $215,000 in accounts receivable for January, 74.4 percent ($160,000/$215,000) are 30 days old or less, 14.0 percent ($30,000/$215,000) are 31 to 60 days old, and 11.6 percent ($25,000/$215,000) are 61 to 90 days old.

Based on the information in this schedule, the unwary manager could erroneously conclude that the collection pattern is steadily worsening. Despite the constant payment pattern assumed in the example, the aging schedule shows the percentage of current receivables falling and the percentage of receivables more than 30 days old increasing. But even though both of the traditional methods of tracking receivables generate misleading information, the basic data needed to track collections accurately are found in them.

TABLE 4-5. XYZ Corporation's Accounts Receivable Aging Schedule

Month	AR	0 to 30 Days	31 to 60 Days	61 to 90 Days
January	$215,000	74.4%	14.0%	11.6%
February	230,000	69.6	26.1	4.3
March	240,000	66.7	25.0	8.3
April	200,000	60.0	30.0	10.0
May	265,000	75.5	17.0	7.5
June	370,000	75.7	20.3	4.0
July	450,000	71.1	23.3	5.6
August	395,000	60.8	30.4	8.8
September	290,000	55.2	31.0	13.8
October	290,000	69.0	20.7	10.3
November	535,000	82.2	14.0	3.8
December	390,000	51.3	42.3	6.4

Payments Pattern Approach

The only way to track accounts receivable accurately is to track actual collections. The payments pattern approach developed by Lewellen and Johnson (1972) involves linking cash collections back to the original sales that generated them. The basic approach is to determine the percentage of each month's sales collected in the month of the sale and the percentages collected in each of the subsequent months.

Table 4-6 shows monthly sales data plus an accounts receivable aging schedule for ABC Corporation. This is all the information needed to generate a report that accurately reflects a customer payment pattern. Table 4-7 shows the payments pattern schedule derived from the data presented in Table 4-6. The entries in Table 4-7 for January are calculated as follows:

January Sales	$1,560
− January Receivables 0 to 30 Days	− (0.743 × $1,575)
= January Sales Collected in January	= $390
January Receivables 0 to 30 Days	(0.743 × $1,575)
− February Receivables 31 to 60 Days	− (0.153 × $1,688)
= January Sales Collected in February	= $912
February Receivables 31 to 60 Days	(0.153 × $1,688)
− March Receivables 61 to 90 Days	− (0.052 × $1,782)
= January Sales Collected in March	= $166
March Receivables 61 to 90 Days	(0.052 × $1,782)
− April Receivables 91 to 120 Days	− 0
= January Sales Collected in April	= $92

Each month's collections are then calculated as a percentage of January's sales volume to arrive at the actual entries in Table 4-7 (e.g., $390/ $1,560 = 25.0%; $912/$1,560 = 58.4%). A close examination of the data in the payment pattern schedule reveals that the stable payment pattern suggested by the accounts receivable aging schedule is slowly deteriorating. The payment pattern schedule reveals that the percentages collected in 0 to 30 and 31 to 60 days are declining and the percentages collected in 61 to 90 and 91 to 120 days are increasing. From this information it is clear that receivables collections are slowing. Care should be taken to ensure that fluctuations in the payments pattern represent a trend, not seasonal or random factors.

The benefits of thoroughly understanding the cash flow process go beyond being able to point out the symptoms of cash flow problems.

TABLE 4-6. ABC Corporation's Monthly Sales Data and Accounts Receivable Aging Schedule

Month	Sales (000s)	EOM AR (000s)	0 to 30 Days	31 to 60 Days	61 to 90 Days
January	$1,560	$1,575	74.3%	18.2%	7.5%
February	1,620	1,688	73.4	15.3	11.3
March	1,750	1,782	75.8	19.0	5.2
April	2,000	2,077	75.9	17.9	6.2
May	2,200	2,380	73.7	20.7	5.6
June	2,050	2,341	69.4	23.2	7.4
July	2,360	2,581	73.2	20.8	6.0
August	2,010	2,404	66.0	27.4	6.6

With little training almost anyone can recognize low or negative cash balances, poor accounts receivable collections, failure to take advantage of discounts, high inventory turnover, and excessive reliance on short-term credit (bank financing and factoring). A working knowledge of the cash flow process helps the analyst, manager, investor, and entrepreneur focus on a system of cash management and control. Of particular importance is the ability to forecast cash requirements and thus the ability to forecast receivables.

INTEGRATIVE APPROACH

The results of some current literature on cash flow analysis indicate that the analysis provides no new information (Casey and Bartczak, 1984, 1985). Other findings indicate that cash flow analysis may be more useful in evaluating the liquidity position of a firm than the traditional ratio

TABLE 4-7. ABC Corporations's Payment Pattern Schedule

Month	0 to 30 Days	31 to 60 Days	61 to 90 Days	91 to 120 Days
January	25.0%	58.4%	10.7%	5.9%
February	23.5	55.6	12.9	8.0
March	22.8	56.0	13.6	7.6
April	21.2	54.2	15.9	8.7
May	20.2	55.1	17.7	7.0
June	20.8	53.0	18.5	7.7
July	19.9	52.2	20.1	7.8
August	21.0	52.5	21.2	5.3

tools (Gentry, Newbold, and Whitford 1985; Gombola and Ketz 1983). In reality, both of these viewpoints are limited. Traditional ratio analysis is just as valid today as it was 50 years ago. Likewise, the new approaches of cash flow analysis seem to hold promise for a richer insight into the financial condition of a firm.

To understand the financial condition of an ongoing business operation fully, an integrative approach using both traditional and cash flow analysis is essential. Accrual-based measures provide information on the profitability of an operation and insights into its solvency. But they cannot measure liquidity and determine financial flexibility adequately. This is the aspect of the analysis that cash flow techniques are uniquely designed to measure. Likewise, the use of cash flow analysis without accrual-based analysis provides an incomplete picture.

SUMMARY

This chapter concentrated on the aspect of liquidity determined by the firm's cash cycle, namely, cash flow from operations. The chapter began by stressing the differences between cash flow and the various definitions of profit. Based on empirical evidence, cash flow measures contain information that is not otherwise available in other measures such as net profit, working capital from operations, and net income plus depreciation.

To analyze the adequacy of cash flow from operations, these measures as well as ratios and other measures are used. From a historical perspective, there are analytical tools developed by Bierman, Sorter and Benston, and Fraser. A cash conversion period analysis has been developed recently by Richards and Laughlin. But there are biases inherent in the cash conversion cycle calculation, namely, DSO bias and accounts receivable aging bias. A payment pattern approach has been developed by Lewellen and Johnson as an alternative method of monitoring cash inflows.

REFERENCES

Bierman, H., Jr. 1960. Measuring financial liquidity. *Accounting Review*: 628–632.

Casey, Cornelius, and Norman Bartczak. 1984. Cash flow—It's not the bottom line. *Harvard Business Review* 62(4):61–65.

———. 1985. Using operating cash flow data to predict financial distress: Some extensions. *Journal of Accounting Research* 23(1):384–401.

Fraser, Lynn M. 1983. Cash flow from operations and liquidity analysis: A new financial ratio for commercial bank lending decisions. *The Journal of Commercial Bank Lending* 66(3):45–52.

Gentry, James A., Paul Newbold, and David T. Whitford. 1985. Predicting bankruptcy: If cash flow's not the bottom line, what is? *Financial Analysts Journal* 41(5):47–54.

Gombola, Michael J., and J. Edward Ketz. 1981a. Alternative measures of cash flow: Part I. *Cashflow* (October): 33–37.

———. 1981b. Alternative measures of cash flow: Part II. *Cashflow* (November): 39–42.

———. 1983. A note on cash flow and classification patterns of financial ratios. *The Accounting Review* 58(1):105–114.

Largay, James A. III, and Clyde P. Stickney. 1980. Cash flows, ratio analysis and the W.T. Grant Company bankruptcy. *Financial Analysts Journal* 36(4): 51–54.

Lewellen, Wilbur G., and Robert W. Johnson. 1972. Better way to monitor accounts receivable. *Harvard Business Review* 50(3):101–109.

Richards, Verlyn D., and Eugene J. Laughlin. 1980. A cash conversion cycle approach to liquidity analysis. *Financial Management* 9(1):32–38.

Sorter, G. H. and George Benston. 1960. Appraising the defensive position of a firm: The interval measure. *The Accounting Review* 35:633–640.

Viscione, Jerry A. 1985. Assessing financial distress. *The Journal of Commercial Bank Lending* 67(11):39–55.

Chapter 5

Liquidity Analysis

Chapter 4 developed several tools for analyzing the operating cash flow portion of the cash flow statement. The operating cash flow position of a firm, however, represents only one aspect of liquidity. This chapter expands the assessment of a firm's liquidity position by developing tools for analyzing cash flow from investing and financing activities.

DEFINING LIQUIDITY

The term *liquidity* brings to mind the relationship of current assets to current liabilities. But liquidity encompasses much more than these two balance sheet accounts. The overall financial structure of a firm has an impact on liquidity, as do a firm's product line, the expertise of its management, and the industry's vitality, among other aspects.

The concept of liquidity can be viewed from two perspectives. The traditional view of liquidity is the time an asset takes to be converted into cash or the time it takes to pay a current liability; in other words, the ability of a firm to pay its bills on time. This approach to liquidity analysis is very short-run and relates to a firm's operating or cash cycle as discussed in Chapter 4.

A broader concept of liquidity addresses a firm's degree of financial flexibility. More specifically, liquidity may be seen as the ability of a firm to augment its future cash flows to cover any unforeseen needs or to take advantage of any unforeseen opportunities.

This second concept of liquidity has been referred to as *financial flexibility* by Campbell, Johnson, and Savoie (1984). This viewpoint, which is much broader, considers things such as a firm's stability of earnings, relative debt to equity position, which can affect its access to external financing sources, and availability of credit lines.

To see management's attitude and perception of liquidity, Campbell,

Johnson, and Savoie surveyed the Fortune 1000 companies; they got a 30% response rate. The survey summarized management's perceptions of the importance of various factors on internal monitoring of liquidity. They found that traditional monitoring of accounts receivable and inventory as well as short-term cash flow projections and good bank relations are seen as extremely valuable tools in the management and planning of corporate liquidity. Perhaps the most important finding of the study is that a traditional method of analyzing financial statements — ratio analysis — is considered a weak tool for monitoring liquidity. It may be safe to say that it is not ratio analysis itself that is weak but rather that ratios have yet to be developed that are effective at measuring the liquidity aspect of a business operation.

To measure and monitor liquidity properly, the standards and approaches used in the past must be discarded and a new framework must be developed. Ludeman (1974) suggests that this new perspective should include the following:

- Amount and trend of internal cash flow
- Aggregate lines of credit and degree of line usage
- Attractiveness to investors of the firm's commercial paper, long-term bonds, and common equity
- Overall expertise of management

From these ideas, it should be obvious that liquidity analysis involves much more than computing the relationship between current assets and current liabilities. Liquidity analysis should consider the overall framework of management's ability to monitor and control the firm's ability to generate operating cash flow.

Traditional Measures of Liquidity

Traditional measures of liquidity actually address the question of solvency rather than liquidity. They are static and measure a firm's ability to pay current debt by liquidating assets. Liquidity ratios taking this approach include:

- Current ratio
- Quick ratio
- Net working capital
- Current liabilities/net worth
- Current liabilities/inventory

- Total liabilities/net worth
- Fixed assets/net worth

Another set of traditional liquidity ratios measures the turnover of a specific activity in a firm's various current asset accounts. These ratios focus on a more dynamic approach, that relates a balance sheet account to a flow such as sales. Examples are dividing sales by the various working capital accounts such as receivables, inventory, and net working capital. These ratios measure the relative speed in which the funds invested in the respective account turn over. The greater the turnover, the more liquid the working capital account. The cash conversion period developed by Richards and Laughlin (1980) is a prime example of this type of analysis.

Impact of Sales Growth on Liquidity

The role of sales growth is important because cash flow can be adversely affected by the growth rate of the company even though the company may be very profitable. Fast growth puts a strain on liquidity that must be managed differently than if liquidity is constrained because of poor profitability or some other reason. Firms with a large market share in a slow growth industry tend to have very strong cash flows (such companies are often referred to as cash cows), whereas firms with a small market share in a rapidly growing industry tend to have very poor operating cash flows.

Determining the rate of sales growth that is compatible with a firm's established financial policies is a key element in understanding liquidity and managing the cash flow cycle. The concept of *sustainable growth* developed by Robert C. Higgins (1977) provides a framework to test whether a firm's growth objectives are contributing to its liquidity problems.

Sustainable growth analysis starts with the premise that there is a certain level of sales growth that can be supported by the internally generated funds of an operation. Firms with growth rates that exceed the sustainable rate will experience difficulties adhering to financial policies and generating enough cash to maintain operations. If a firm is not generating sufficient cash flow from operations to support its rate of growth, other sources of financing must be identified. Firms that grow faster than the sustainable rate must support their growth through cash generated from investing or financing activities, that is, by selling fixed assets, issuing new debt, or selling additional equity shares. This will often result in violating established financial policies. Firms growing at rates below the sustainable rate will have surplus cash to build an asset base, pay off debt, or possibly increase dividend payout.

A firm's future growth potential is dependent on its total asset base.

In other words, total assets must increase more or less proportionately with sales or there will be a negative impact on the firm's long-term ability to grow. In addition, creditors often impose external restrictions on an operation in the form of financial covenants in loan contracts and shareholders place a high value on the payment of dividends. These restrictions will dictate certain target values for various ratios, for example, sales-to-total assets, debt-to-equity, and dividends-to-earnings ratios.

Following Higgins' approach, sustainable growth can be estimated by equating annual sources of capital to annual uses. First, define the following parameters:

$S =$ Level of sales at the beginning of the year

$gS =$ Change in sales during the year, where g is the growth rate for sales and S is defined above

$A/S =$ Target ratio of total-assets-to-total-sales

$m =$ Projected after-tax profit margin

$d =$ Target dividend payout ratio; that is, ratio of dividends to earnings

$D/E =$ Target debt-to-equity ratio

If sales are to increase by gS, then assets must grow proportionately to keep A/S constant. In other words, sales growth of gS will require an addition to the asset base of $gS(A/S)$, which represents a use of capital.

Sources of capital originate from the liabilities and equity side of the balance sheet. Additions to retained earnings will be net profit minus dividends paid. This is depicted by the expression $[m \times (S + gS) \times (1 - d)]$. As equity increases by this amount, liabilities can increase proportionately and still maintain a constant value for D/E. The expression for the increase in liabilities is $[m \times (S + gS) \times (1 - d) \times (D/E)]$.

Total uses must equal total sources. Equating the two results gives the following:

$$gS \times (A/S) = m \times (S + gS) \times (1 - d) \\ + m \times (S + gS) \times (1 - d) \times (D/E)$$

The growth rate for sales, g, that satisfies the above equality is defined as the sustainable growth rate:

$$g = \frac{m \times (1 - d) \times [1 + (D/E)]}{A/S - \{m \times (1 - d) \times [1 + (D/E)]\}}$$

The critical operating variable in the equation is the addition to retained earnings, the major spontaneous source of cash in this framework. One could argue that if earnings retention is not sufficient to support the growth objectives of a firm, new equity could be issued. This argument, however, ignores the nonspontaneous aspect of new equity issues and the fact that conditions in equity markets may not be conducive to new issues when funds are needed.

Table 5-1 summarizes the relevant parameters for Chrysler from 1984 to 1986. Substituting these parameter values into the sustainable growth equation results in values for g of 217, 56, and 30 percent for the 3 years, respectively. The calculation for 1986 follows. Calculations for the other years are done in a similar manner.

$$g = \frac{0.0621 \times (1 - 0.1256) \times (1 + 1.71)}{0.6404 - [0.0621 \times (1 - 0.1256) \times (1 + 1.71)]}$$

$$= \frac{0.1472}{0.4932} = 29.85 \text{ percent}$$

Chrysler's actual sales growth rates were significantly below these values. This is a favorable position to be in and implies that the company has sufficient capital to meet its operating needs. As a result of the flexibility offered by the relatively low growth rates, Chrysler was able to increase its asset base aggressively, increase its dividend payout rate, and simultaneously improve its liquidity position. W.T. Grant, on the other hand, had sales growth in 1973 and 1974 of 19.6 and 12.5 percent, respectively. Sustainable growth for those same years were 5.2 and −3.8 percent, respectively. Grant declared bankruptcy in 1975.

As in the case with Chrysler, firms are not able to control financial ratios from one year to the next. But even though there is considerable variation, the ratios can be used effectively in determining how fast a firm can expand without changing the ownership structure, the dividend payout rate, or other financial characteristics of the operation.

TABLE 5-1. Chrysler's Sustainable Growth Parameters

Parameter	1984	1985	1986
m	0.1207	0.0759	0.0621
d	0.0508	0.0709	0.1256
D/E	1.74	1.99	1.71
A/S	0.4587	0.5848	0.6404

LIQUIDITY INDICES

The development of liquidity analysis can be traced through the use of ratios or indices as the analysis has progressed from the original measure of liquidity, the current ratio. During the last 30 years, various liquidity ratios have been proposed that relate to one another.

One of the first ratios developed is the ratio of current assets to current liabilities, commonly referred to as the current ratio. Its origin can be traced to the early 1900s. Although the current ratio has always been viewed as a liquidity measure, its approach to liquidity ignores the going-concern aspect of the firm. Rather it indicates the degree of coverage that short-term creditors have if current assets were to be liquidated to pay off the current liabilities. Liquidating current assets to pay off current maturing liabilities would obviously disrupt the operating cycle of a firm and is clearly not an option unless the firm is being liquidated.

In an article that broke with this traditional viewpoint of liquidity, Walter (1957) looked at liquidity from a viewpoint of technical solvency. This concept goes beyond that of the current and related ratios in that it takes a going-concern approach. For example, the current ratio stresses the availability of current assets with which to discharge a firm's current liabilities. Walter's approach is concerned with whether cash inflows plus liquid resources such as cash and marketable securities cover cash requirements by a sufficient margin so as to protect a firm against unforeseen variations in cash resources or requirements.

Walter suggests that liquidity analysis be expanded to include analysis of profitability, net cash flows, source and use of funds statement, and trends in sales. He indicates that the higher a firm's level of profitability, as measured by the profit-to-sales ratio, the smaller the liquidity risk associated with any given working capital position.

A study conducted by Lemke (1970) found that when sales are varied, but the efficiency of working capital management and the firm's liquidity are held constant, the current ratio exhibits one of several patterns. Thus, neither the absolute level nor the trend of the current ratio or any of its related variations such as the quick ratio can be given a consistent interpretation. He concluded that the fundamental deficiency of the current ratio is that it ignores cash flow and focuses entirely on static balances. An index of liquidity ideally should consider cash inflows as well as cash outflows over a future planning period.

Through his concern for the inadequacies of the traditional measures of liquidity such as the current ratio, Lemke developed a *liquidity flow index* (LFI), which overcomes the deficiencies of the traditional static measures. Its basic form is

$$LFI = \frac{\text{Practical Maximum Rate of Cash Outflow}}{\text{Required Rate of Cash Outflow}}$$

Lemke defined the numerator as the total dollar amount of cash available over a given time period to meet required outflows without temporarily drawing on long-term funds or compromising future operating efficiency. This would include cash inflow during the period, beginning cash and liquid balances minus required ending balances needed to maintain adequate liquidity, plus net additional funds raised during the period for noncurrent purposes.

The denominator consists of the dollar amount of cash obligations over the indicated planning period, including operating expenses, payments for fixed assets, and scheduled debt repayments.

Lemke stressed that a variation of this index, the projected liquidity flow index, overcomes all the deficiencies of the traditional static liquidity measures. This measure would include expected future cash flows as well as liquid balances.

An LFI measure for a properly managed firm should be close to 1.00. An LFI consistently over 1.00 would signal an inefficient or ultra-conservatively managed firm. An index below 1.00 would signal an illiquid firm.

The greatest shortcoming of the Lemke LFI measure is the rather extreme data requirements. Many components of the numerator and denominator could only be reasonably estimated internally by corporate management. As such, it seems to be a relevant measure for internal management but nearly impossible to use by external analysts.

An interesting ratio developed by Gale and Branch (1981) is a useful tool for helping corporations manage their strategic investment in various divisions:

$$\frac{\text{Cash Reinvested (Increase in Gross Plant and Equipment Plus Increase in Net Working Capital)}}{\text{Cash Generated (After-Tax Income Plus Depreciation)}}$$

Businesses in rapidly growing markets usually have cash reinvestment ratios greater than 1.00, whereas those in declining or slow-growth markets have ratios much less than 1.00. As mentioned, a ratio such as this can be useful in allocating funds among various divisions. For example, investment in a division in a high-growth area may need to be offset with investments in lower growth areas so that the corporation does not find itself in a severe liquidity crisis.

In a study conducted by Gombola and Ketz (1983), a factor loading analysis of a group of 40 financial ratios was conducted. The study concluded that when cash flow is approximated by using net income plus depreciation and amortization, the subsequent "cash flow" ratios closely correspond to profitability measures. When cash flow is measured as operating cash revenues less operating cash expenses, however, the resulting cash flow ratios load on a separate and distinct factor that is not captured by any other ratio group.

The cash flow ratios they developed for their study consisted of the following:

CFFO/equity   Type of cash flow return on equity
CFFO/sales   Cash flow profit margin concept
CFFO/total assets Cash flow asset turnover ratio
CFFO/total debt   Type of coverage ratio

It is important to stress that each of the above ratios has an accrual-based counterpart and that the cash flow based ratios appear to provide a distinctly different set of information.

Emery (1984) published a study that developed a liquidity measure from a function of the likelihood that a firm will exhaust its liquid reserve. Their measure consists of three parts. First, firms rely on a stock of liquid resources that can be quickly converted into cash without impairing the operations of the firm. Examples of liquid resources are cash, marketable securities, and lines of credit. The second component is the level of cash flow from operations expected over the planning horizon. The final component is a measure of the variability of the expected cash flow from operations.

Together, the three components form a liquidity index they called lambda:

$$\text{Lambda} = \frac{\text{Initial Liquid Reserve} + \text{Total Anticipated Net Cash Flow During Analysis Horizon}}{\text{Uncertainty About Net Cash Flow During Analysis Horizon}}$$

The denominator is the standard deviation of the distribution of a firm's expected cash flow from operations. If future cash flows are expected to be similar to past cash flows, historical data can be used to assess the future cash flow.

Lambda represents the first attempt at incorporating information about the distribution of operating cash flow into a liquidity measure. It is very appealing because a firm with a relatively low liquid balance and moderate cash flows may be just as liquid as a firm with a large liquid reserve and above-average positive cash flows if the cash flows of the firm with the low liquid reserves are much more certain. In other words, liquid reserves are only needed to meet unforeseen circumstances that come about when there is a high degree of uncertainty regarding future events. If the future is relatively stable, the need for significant liquidity reserves diminishes.

Shulman and Cox (1985) developed an extension to the cash conversion period concept developed by Richards and Laughlin (1980) as discussed in Chapter 4. Their basic contribution was to add new interpretations to various working capital relationships.

First they observed that the traditional definition of net working capital (NWC), that is, current assets (CA) − current liabilities (CL), was not reflective of its real impact on liquidity. They offered an alternative interpretation that equated NWC to the difference between permanent capital (PC) (long-term liabilities and net worth) and net fixed assets (NFA). From this viewpoint, the dollar amount of positive net working capital measures that portion of current assets financed with permanent funds. A negative level of net working capital indicates that portion of current liabilities financing net fixed assets. These relationships are shown in Figure 5-1.

To expand their analysis further, Shulman and Cox created two new definitions. First, they defined *working capital requirements* (WCR) as the difference between current operating assets, which consists of prepaids, inventory and receivables, and current operating liabilities defined as payables and accruals. These accounts represent spontaneous uses and sources of funds over a firm's operating cycle.

They then defined *net liquid balance* (NLB) as the difference between current financial assets such as cash and marketable securities and current financial liabilities such as notes payable and current maturing debt. Note the relationship between WCR, NLB, and NWC:

$$NWC = WCR + NLB$$

The NLB serves as their proposed measure of liquidity. To see how NLB measures liquidity, remember the interpretation of a positive level of NWC. It is the dollar amount of current assets financed by permanent capital. Over the operating cycle of the firm, the dollar amount of positive working capital requirements, which is a component of NWC, will expand as sales expand and will contract as sales contract. During

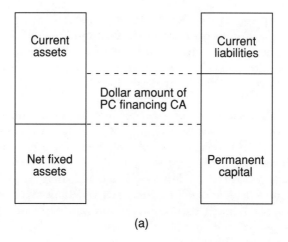

(a)

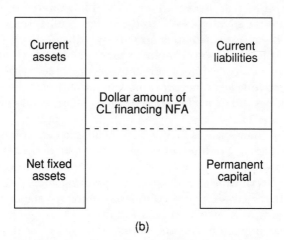

(b)

Figure 5-1. Alternative interpretation of NWC
(a) Operations with positive NWC (b) Operations
with negative NWC.

the upswing, the expanding dollar amount of WCR must either be
financed by drawing down the NLB, adding to permanent capital by
acquiring new long-term debt or equity financing, or both. Therefore,
the more positive the NLB, the greater financial flexibility the firm has
to finance its working capital requirements.

In addition, the greater the degree of profitability, the more liquidity
the firm has because that will spontaneously add to the permanent capital

base of the firm. If the increase in WCR is seasonal, drawing down the net liquid balance is appropriate. If the increase in WCR is permanent because of a new higher level of operations, however, the increase in WCR should be financed with a permanent source of funds in order to maintain the firm's level of liquidity.

The absolute dollar NLB balance may be used as a measure of a firm's liquidity. If the measure is negative, it indicates a dependence on outside financing and is indicative of the minimum borrowing line required. Although a negative NLB does not by itself suggest that a firm is going to default on its debt obligations, it does imply that the firm has reduced financial flexibility.

The absolute dollar NLB balance can also be measured on a relative basis by dividing NLB by total assets. The greater this ratio, the greater the liquidity. The NLB can also be converted to a days sales basis so as to tie in with the cash conversion period developed by Richards and Laughlin. On this basis, liquidity could be measured by the number of days sales in the net liquid balance or the number of days sales tied up in the firm's working capital requirements.

Using working capital requirements as an index of working capital needs, Hawawini, Viallet, and Vora (HVV) (1986) performed a comparison of the working capital policies across industries. Their reason for using WCR was that net working capital contains some components that are not closely related to a firm's operating cycle. The working capital requirements approach is useful because the traditional net working capital figure includes accounts not directly related to the operating cycle. For example, the cash account, the marketable securities account, and the notes payable balance should be viewed as balances resulting from internal financial decisions or policies, not balances resulting from the operating cycle of the firm. They should therefore be excluded from consideration.

The approach of HVV is consistent with the decomposition of net working capital into net liquid balance and working capital requirements developed by Shulman and Cox (1985). HVV standardized WCR by dividing it by sales, thereby developing a working capital requirements to sales ratio, or WCR/S. They found that this ratio was statistically different across industry categories, indicating that industries have significantly different working capital needs. All other factors constant, the greater this ratio, the greater reliance a company will have on external funds given a change in sales. Thus, the larger the WCR/S ratio, the less financial flexibility and less liquidity the firm will have because its operating cycle will require significant investment of funds. In cases in which WCR is negative, a firm's operating cycle becomes a permanent source of financing, and the positive impact on liquidity will be significant.

The WCR/S ratio suggested by HVV can be modified to include another dimension of liquidity. The impact of a large WCR/S ratio can be offset by a high profit margin. It can be shown that the impact on required nonspontaneous financing by the level of WCR for a given change in the sales growth rate is equal to

$$\text{WCR Pressure Ratio} = \text{WCR/S} - [m \times (1 - d)]$$

where m is net profit divided by sales and d is the dividend payout ratio. The smaller this ratio, the more liquid the firm and the less financial pressure exerted by the working capital cycle. This type of liquidity measure was actually hinted at by Walter (1957) but was not developed.

FRAMEWORK FOR LIQUIDITY ANALYSIS

This section develops an integrative approach to the assessment of liquidity. It shows that the change in the net liquid balance results from the interaction of three different cash flow measures — cash flow from operations, cash from investing activities, and new permanent capital. The more dependent a firm is on obtaining external capital to fund its operations, that is, the greater the imbalance between cash flow from operations and new permanent capital, the less liquid the firm is due to its reliance on nonspontaneous sources of funds that are beyond its control.

The Shulman–Cox net liquid balance liquidity analysis can be expanded into a more dynamic assessment of liquidity. Table 5-2 presents a simplified cash flow statement showing that the change in the net liquid balance between two operating periods is a function of a firm's level of cash flow from operations less the cash flow related to investment activities plus new permanent capital. The terms on the right-hand side of the equation at the bottom of Table 5-2 can be collected to form two categories, cash flow from operations (CFFO) and new long-term permanent capital net of dividends paid (NPC) minus cash flow from investing activities (CFFI). These relationships form the following expression for the change in NLB:

$$\Delta \text{NLB} = \text{CFFO} + [\text{NPC} - \text{CFFI}]$$

The expression represents a dynamic reformulation of the NLB concept developed by Shulman and Cox (1985). It shows that the change in the level of liquidity, as evidenced by the change in the net liquid balance, Δ NLB, is a function of cash flow from operations, the addition

TABLE 5-2. Simplified Statement of Cash Flow Using the Direct Approach

Plus:	Sales
Minus:	Δ accounts receivable
Equal:	Operating cash receipts
Minus:	Cost of goods sold
Plus:	Δ accounts payable and accruals
Minus:	Δ inventory
Minus:	Interest expense
Equal:	Cash flow from operations
Minus:	Cash flow from investing activities (CFFI)
Plus:	New permanent financing (long-term debt and equity)
Minus:	Dividends
Equal:	Δ net liquid balance

Δ NLB = CFFO − CFFI + new permanent financing − dividends

of permanent capital net of dividends paid, and level of investment. This one equation brings together short-term aspects of liquidity related to current cash generation and long-term aspects of financial flexibility represented by the interaction between the change in permanent capital (NPC) and cash flow from investing activities (CFFI).

The net liquid balance can either increase or decrease because of the basic cases developed in Table 5-3. Cases 1 through 3 are defined to have a positive change in NLB; Cases 4 through 6 are defined to have a negative change in NLB.

Case 1 represents the best level of liquidity because NLB increases due to positive cash flow and a positive level of net permanent financing. The positive change in NLB in case 2 results from positive cash flow that exceeds the investment in plant net of permanent capital. Case 3 results from a negative cash flow, which is offset by a net inflow of permanent financing. It is not clear whether case 2 or 3 is more liquid since liquidity is not only a function of cash flow but also of the ability to access the financial markets as well.

Cases 4, 5, and 6 have negative changes in NLB. Case 4 is characterized by positive cash flow, which is more than absorbed by a net investment in plant. Case 5 has negative cash flow that exceeds the net permanent financing obtained. Again, a priori, it is not clear whether case 4 or 5 is more liquid. Finally, case 6, the least liquid one, has a negative cash flow, with the net investment in plant financed by drawing down the net liquid balance.

It has been clearly shown that the change in NLB is not only due to

TABLE 5-3. Factors Affecting Change in Net Liquid Balance

Change in NLB	CFFO	NPC − CFFI
Case 1		
(+)	(+)	(+)

The NLB increases because operating cash flow is positive and new permanent capital exceeds the dollar amount of capital expenditures. This would be a condition of excess liquidity and an inappropriate use of permanent capital. Permanent capital along with an excess of cash flow is being invested in short-term liquidity.

Case 2		
(+)	(+)	(−)

The NLB increases. Capital expenditures are incrementally funded by operating cash flows. This would signal more than adequate liquidity and that the firm is not using up its financial flexibility. Cash flow funds help fund capital expenditures, with the residual building up the net liquid balance.

Case 3		
(+)	(−)	(+)

The NLB increases even though CFFO is negative because new permanent capital exceeds the dollar level of capital expenditures. This should be taken as a warning of future liquidity problems. Liquidity is based on the firm's ability to obtain external capital.

Case 4		
(−)	(+)	(−)

Operating cash flow is positive, but there is not enough to cover the excess of capital expenditures over the new permanent capital obtained. The firm is in essence funding a part of its capital expenditures with short-term funds.

Case 5		
(−)	(−)	(+)

The NLB declines. Operating cash flow is negative and absorbs the net surplus of new permanent capital over capital expenditures. The firm is mortgaging its financial flexibility because of its poor cash flow performance.

Case 6		
(−)	(−)	(−)

This is the worst case. The firm is using short-term funds to cover its cash flow deficiency and the excess of capital expenditures over new permanent capital.

cash flow from operations but also to *cash flow from financing* and *investing activities.* In an article about W.T. Grant, Largay and Stickney (1980) only analyzed cash flow from operations. Liquidity analysis that focuses only on operating cash flow ignores two potentially important categories of cash flow that have an impact on the liquidity position of a firm.

Integrative Framework

It is still unclear how the ratios presented here and in Chapter 4 relate to one another and how to use them to perform an analysis of liquidity and, more specifically, to analyze the new statement of cash flow. A framework based on the relationship of the components of the change in the net liquid balance is needed.

To devise such a framework, the COMPUSTAT™ database was used to select industrial firms with SIC codes from 1000 to 6000 for 1971, 1976, and 1981. A sample of liquidity measures was then calculated for the chosen firms. Each firm with its corresponding ratios was then sorted by the case each firm represented based on an analysis of the components of the change in net liquid balance. Then the mean values, by case, were calculated for the sample of liquidity ratios analyzed. Table 5-4 presents the mean values, by case, for both the change in the net liquid balance and its components and the ratios studied.

Figures 5-2 through 5-4 graphically present the mean values for the change in the net liquid balance and its cash flow components for the sample of firms studied. These figures will provide a point of reference as each liquidity ratio is discussed.

The first ratio to be analyzed is the liquidity ratio developed by Fraser (1983). The Fraser ratio shown in Figure 5-5 corresponds closely to the operating cash flow component. Comparing the ratio to the graph of the operating cash flow component in Figure 5-3 demonstrates that it is heavily influenced by the direction of cash flow from operations. The lowest values for the Fraser ratio occur in cases that experience negative operating cash flow. The mean values for the Fraser ratio for the three time periods studied are significantly different across most of the six cases. The systematic variation is due to CFFO. When CFFO is positive, the Fraser ratio is high (cases 1, 2, and 4); when it is negative, the Fraser ratio is low (cases 3, 5, and 6).

The Fraser ratio ranks liquidity based on operating cash flow. Even though the change in net liquid balance is negative in case 4, the Fraser ratio is greater than its mean value for case 3, in which the change in net liquid balance is positive. For all 3 years, the mean value of the Fraser ratio for case 4 exceeds its mean value for case 3. If this ratio is an accurate measure of liquidity, the ranking of the cases in descending order of liquidity based on the mean values of the ratio would be in the following order: case 2, case 4, case 1, case 6, case 3, case 5.

The Sorter–Benston cash interval ratio is shown in Figure 5-6. The general trend is for the cash interval to decline from case 1 to case 6, which is generally consistent with the interpretation that case 1 is the most liquid case and case 6 is the least liquid case. In general, however,

TABLE 5-4. Mean Values by Case for Components of the Change in NLB and for Selected Ratios (Millions of dollars)

1981 Ratio	Case					
	1	2	3	4	5	6
Sample size	100	563	66	547	68	131
Change in NLB	$49.30	$ 28.96	$42.29	-$ 63.09	-$10.73	-$34.76
CFFO	$31.47	$121.97	-$23.32	$150.48	-$21.75	-$13.69
NPC − CFFI	$17.83	-$ 93.01	$65.38	-$213.57	$11.02	-$21.06
Fraser	0.68	0.84	-.03	0.75	-0.36	0.18
WCR/S − $m \times (1 - d)$	0.23	0.19	0.30	0.18	0.33	0.31
Short-term debt/total liability	0.089	0.086	0.089	0.117	0.186	0.239
Current ratio	2.88	2.38	2.86	2.03	2.33	1.96
S-B cash interval (days)	81.56	29.37	45.65	19.44	13.39	23.09
TL/NW	1.14	1.22	1.58	1.49	1.96	1.60
ROA (%)	6.61	6.76	3.96	5.51	2.40	2.47
Cash conversion period (days)	122	107	154	96	156	166

1976 Ratio	Case					
	1	2	3	4	5	6
Sample size	92	648	55	428	49	113
Change in NLB	$28.52	$ 35.39	$ 3.90	-$15.78	-$1.86	-$17.05
CFFO	$18.60	$104.79	-$ 7.23	$44.88	-$3.69	-$ 7.30
NPC − CFFI	$ 9.92	-$ 69.44	$11.14	-$60.67	$1.83	-$ 9.75
Fraser	0.59	1.00	-0.02	0.83	-0.15	0.16
WCR/S − $m \times (1 - d)$	0.26	0.19	0.29	0.19	0.38	0.28

Short-term debt/total liability	0.102	0.078	0.099	0.141	0.162	0.254
Current ratio	2.75	2.51	2.68	2.21	2.59	2.12
S-B cash interval (days)	46.91	40.67	18.98	22.46	23.71	16.05
TL/NW	1.19	1.16	1.27	1.38	1.49	1.52
ROA (%)	5.17	6.79	4.24	5.44	1.37	2.56
Cash conversion period (days)	138	111	151	107	164	132

1971 Ratio	Case					
	1	2	3	4	5	6
Sample size	142	542	66	348	50	85
Change in NLB	$16.73	$23.09	$4.50	−$10.77	−$2.93	−$10.02
CFFO	$10.89	$68.60	−$5.90	$33.11	−$5.12	−$4.38
NPC − CFFI	$6.05	−$45.51	$10.41	−$43.88	$2.18	−$5.64
Fraser	0.53	0.94	0.00	0.75	−0.19	0.33
$WCR/S - m \times (1 - d)$	0.27	0.24	0.36	0.24	0.37	0.33
Short-term debt/total liability	0.114	0.123	0.114	0.169	0.251	0.273
Current ratio	2.89	2.60	2.91	2.26	2.32	2.32
S-B cash interval (days)	38.80	35.14	64.66	23.06	33.41	21.14
TL/NW	1.37	1.10	1.49	1.11	1.46	1.53
ROA (%)	4.18	5.43	2.94	4.38	2.62	2.27
Cash conversion period (days)	130	125	191	126	164	152

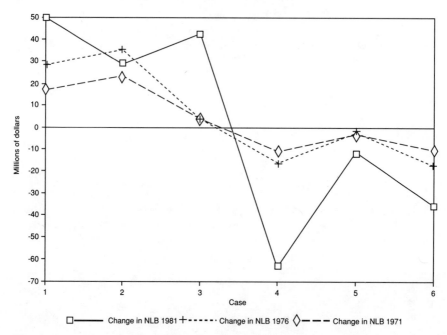

Figure 5-2. Change in NLB by case: □, 1981; +, 1976; ◇, 1971.

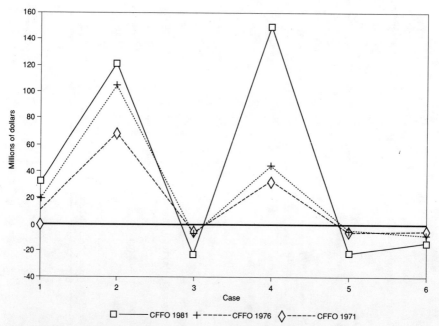

Figure 5-3. CFFO by case: □, 1981; +, 1976; ◇, 1971.

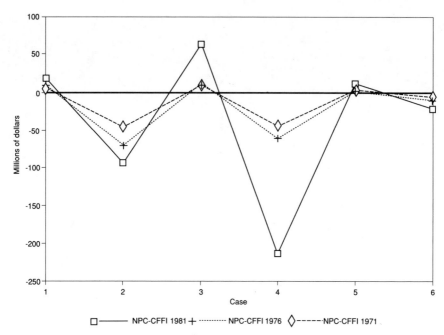

Figure 5-4. New permanent capital—CFFI: □, 1981; +, 1976; ◇, 1971.

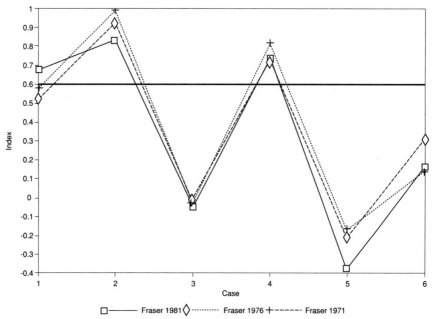

Figure 5-5. Fraser ratio by case: □, 1981; +, 1976; ◇, 1971.

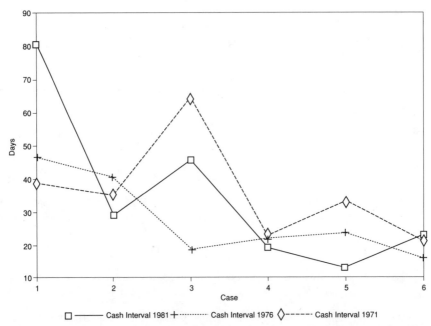

Figure 5-6. Sorter–Benston cash interval ratio by case: □, 1981; +, 1976; ◇, 1971.

the mean values of this ratio for the six liquidity cases are not significantly different nor is there a strong consistent trend among the three time periods observed.

The working capital pressure ratio, reported in Figure 5-7, displays a very strong and consistent pattern for each time period studied. The ratio demonstrates that pressure is exerted in the same cases that experience a negative cash flow, specifically cases 3, 5, and 6. In addition, the mean values for many of the cases are significantly different. Thus, even though this ratio is accrual-based, it seems to be sensitive to cash flow and the liquidity position of the firm. Its ordering of liquidity is similar to the Fraser ratio.

According to the working capital pressure ratio, the most liquid cases are cases 2, 4, and 1, in that order. The least liquid cases are cases 3, 6, and 5, with case 5 being the least liquid. In general, the mean values for the least liquid cases are significantly different from the values for the liquid cases.

The cash conversion period (CCP) behaves in a similar fashion to the working capital pressure ratio. Its mean value for each case is shown in Figure 5-8. The lower the value of the cash conversion period, generally the more liquid the enterprise since spontaneously generated sources are

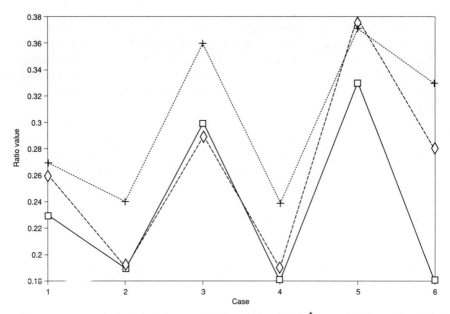

Figure 5-7. Working capital pressure by case: □, 1981; +, 1976; ◇, 1971.

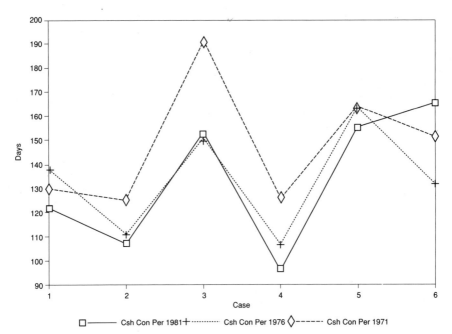

Figure 5-8. Cash conversion period: □, 1981; +, 1976; ◇, 1971.

funding a greater portion of the firm's working capital requirements. Cases 1, 2, and 4 have low mean values for the cash conversion period relative to cases 3, 5, and 6. This ratio, like the Fraser and working capital pressure ratios, seems to be linked to cash flow from operations. The cases with low mean values are those with positive operating cash flows.

Another accrual-based liquidity ratio does not fare as well. Figure 5-9 displays the trend for the current ratio across the six cases for each time period. The current ratio signals that liquidity is highest, based on mean values of the ratio, in cases 1 and 3. In case 3, cash flow is negative. In fact, the current ratio appears to be negatively correlated with the cash flow pattern, the Fraser ratio, and the working capital pressure ratio. This result would seem to be disconcerting since the current ratio has long been billed as a liquidity measure. Comparing Figures 5-9 and 5-3 indicates that the current ratio is relatively high when operating cash flow is negative and relatively low when operating cash flow is positive.

Comparing the trend of the current ratio to the trend in net permanent financing in Figure 5-4, it is apparent that a distinct positive relationship exists. Thus, the current ratio appears to be responding to the

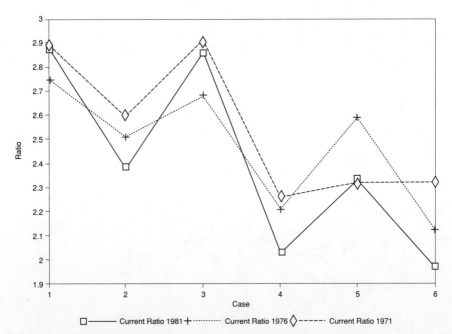

Figure 5-9. Current ratio by case: □, 1981; +, 1976; ◇, 1971.

net impact of financing activities over asset investment activities, whereas the Fraser and working capital pressure ratios appear to respond more to the pattern of cash flow from operations.

Another ratio included in the analysis is the percentage of short-term liabilities to total liabilities. The trend for this ratio is reported in Figure 5-10. For cases 1, 2, and 3, the percentages are reasonably constant and low, with the mean values not significantly different from each other. The mean values increase for each succeeding case, however, and become significantly different from cases 1, 2, and 3. Thus it appears as though an increasing reliance on short-term debt is consistent with decreasing liquidity.

A leverage ratio, measured by total liabilities to net worth, is shown in Figure 5-11. It displays a slight increasing trend moving from case 1 to case 6, but the difference in mean values for the ratios is not generally significant between the cases. Whereas the leverage ratio is generally trending upward, the profitability ratio, shown in Figure 5-12, is trending downward from case 1 to case 6. This would indicate some linkage between profitability and liquidity such that as liquidity declines so does profitability.

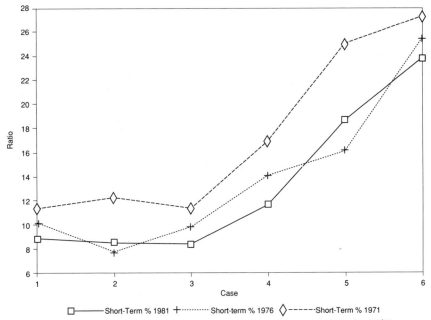

Figure 5-10. Short-term debt ratio by case: □, 1981; +, 1976; ◇, 1971.

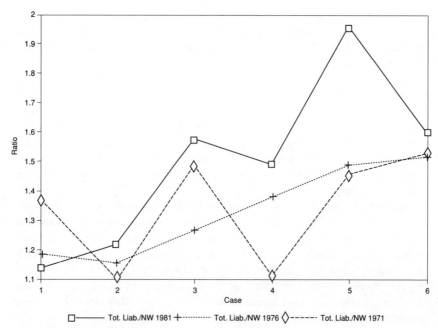

Figure 5-11. Total liabilities to net worth by case: □, 1981; +, 1976; ◇, 1971.

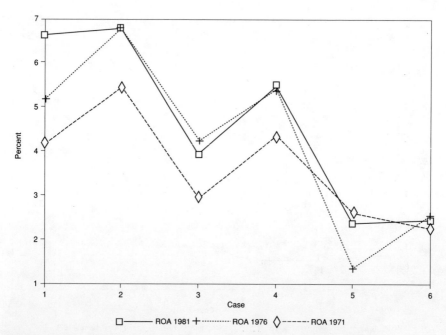

Figure 5-12. Return on assets by case: □, 1981; +, 1976; ◇, 1971.

SUMMARY

A liquidity analysis approach can be developed from two perspectives. The first identifies the direction of change in the net liquid balance, and the second investigates the relationship between the factors causing the change. Using this approach, some of the major liquidity ratios developed during the last 30 years were compared to six cases defining the change in the net liquid balance. It was discovered that the liquidity ratios can be categorized in two general groups: those sensitive to the operating cash flow component and those sensitive to the net permanent financing component.

REFERENCES

Campbell, et. al. 1989. Cash flow, liquidity, and financial flexibility. *Financial Executive* 52(8):14–17.

Emery, Gary W. 1984. Measuring short-term liquidity. *Journal of Cash Management* 3(9):25–32.

Fraser, Lynn M. 1983. Cash flow from operations and liquidity analysis: A new financial ratio for commercial lending decisions. *The Journal of Commercial Bank Lending* 66(3):45–52.

Gale, Bradley, and Ben Branch. 1981. Cash flow analysis: More important than ever. *Harvard Business Review* 59(4):131–136.

Gombola, Michael, and J. Edward Ketz. 1983. A note on cash flow and classification patterns of financial ratios. *The Accounting Review* 58(1):105–114.

Hawawini, Gabriel, Claude Viallet, and Ashok Vora. 1986. Industry influence on corporate working capital decisions. *Sloan Management Review* 27(4):15–24.

Higgins, Robert C. 1977. How much growth can a firm afford? *Financial Management* 6(3):7–16.

Largay, James A. III, and Clyde P. Stickney. 1980. Cash flows, ratio analysis, and the W.T. Grant Company bankruptcy. *Financial Analysts Journal* 36(4):51–54.

Lemke, Kenneth W. 1970. The evaluation of liquidity: An analytical study. *Journal of Accounting Research* (spring):47–77.

Ludeman, Douglas H. 1974. Corporate liquidity in perspective. *Financial Executive* 42(10):18–22.

Richards, Verlyn D., and Eugene J. Laughlin. 1980. A cash conversion cycle approach to liquidity analysis. *Financial Management* 9(1):32–38.

Shulman, Joel M., and Raymond A. K. Cox. 1985. An integrative approach to working capital management. *Journal of Cash Management* 5(6):64–67.

Walter, James, 1957. Determination of technical solvency. *Journal of Business* (January):30–43.

APPENDIX 5A: STATISTICAL TESTS FOR DIFFERENCES BETWEEN MEANS

In order for analysts to make a reasonable assessment of liquidity, they need to know how liquidity measures relate to one another. The framework to determine this relationship is the six cases presented in Table 5-4. The data are a sample of industrial firms based on SIC codes between 1000 and 6000 taken from the COMPUSTAT™ tapes for 1971, 1976, and 1981. The empirical methodology is an analysis of variance of the change in net liquid balance and its components to see if the mean values of the variables are significantly different among the six cases. Tests are made to see if the mean values for the liquidity ratios discussed earlier for a large sample of industrial firms are significantly different among the six cases.

A one-way analysis of variance technique is used to test the difference of means among the six cases of liquidity. Shulman and Cox identified an indicator of liquidity as a positive net liquid balance and of illiquidity as a negative net liquid balance.

This analysis carries that concept one step further by analyzing the change in NLB and the components that cause a change in it. Two such components are CFFO and net permanent financing.

The empirical methodology involves testing for significant differences among the means of the change in net liquid balance, CFFO, and net permanent financing for the six cases. Initial results indicated that the mean values for each of the components was significantly different for the six cases at the 1 percent level of significance. The mean values were presented in Table 5-4.

Next, the Scheffe test was used to see which cases contained the significantly different mean values. It is the most conservative and appropriate test for cases that have unequal sample sizes. The results are shown in Table 5A-1. Here is an example to illustrate how to read the table. In 1981, case 1 contained a sample of 100 firms. The mean value for the change in NLB for the firms in case 1 was significantly different from the mean values for the firms in cases 4 and 6. The results indicate that the mean values for positive changes in NLB are generally significantly different from the mean values of negative changes in NLB.

A second phase in the empirical analysis involved testing the differences in mean values for the liquidity ratios discussed earlier. The results are also displayed in Table 5A-1. The analysis of variance test indicated

TABLE 5A-1. Significance Tests for Differences in Mean Values between Cases for 1981, 1976, and 1971

1981 Ratio	Case					
	1	2	3	4	5	6
Sample size	100	563	66	547	68	131
Change NLB	4, 6	4, 6	4	1, 2, 3		1, 2
CFFO		6	4	3, 5, 6	4	2, 4
NPC − CFFI	4	4	4	1, 2, 3, 5, 6	4	4
Fraser	3, 5, 6	3, 5, 6	1, 2, 4	3, 5, 6	1, 2, 4, 6	1, 2, 4, 5
WCR/S − m × (1 − d)	5, 6	3, 5, 6	2, 4	3, 5, 6	1, 2, 4	1, 2, 4
Short-term debt/total liability	5, 6	4, 5, 6	5, 6	2, 5, 6	1, 2, 3, 4	1, 2, 3, 4
Current ratio	2, 4, 5, 6	1, 3, 4, 6	2, 4, 6	1, 2, 3	1	1, 2, 3
Cash interval	2, 3, 4, 5, 6	1	1, 4, 5	1, 3	1, 3	1
TL/NW	5	5			1, 2	
ROA	5, 6	3, 4, 5, 6	2	2, 5, 6	1, 2, 4	1, 2, 4
Cash conversion period		5, 6	4	3, 5, 6	2, 4	2, 4

1976 Ratio	Case					
	1	2	3	4	5	6
Sample size	92	648	55	428	49	113
Change NLB	4, 6	4, 6		1, 2		1, 2
CFFO		4, 6		2		2
NPC − CFFI	2	1				
Fraser	2, 3, 5, 6	1, 3, 4, 5, 6	1, 2, 4	2, 3, 5, 6	1, 2, 4	1, 2, 4
WCR/S − m × (1 − d)	2, 4, 5	1, 3, 5, 6	2, 4	1, 3, 5, 6	1, 2, 4, 6	2, 4, 5
Short-term debt/total liability	6	4, 5, 6	6	2, 6	2, 6	1, 2, 3, 4, 5

TABLE 5A-1. (Continued)

1976 Ratio	Case					
	1	2	3	4	5	6
Current ratio	4, 6	4, 6		1, 2		1, 2
Cash interval	4, 6	4, 6		1, 2		1, 2
TL/NW						
ROA	5, 6	3, 4, 5, 6	2	2, 5, 6	1, 2, 4	1, 2, 4
Cash conversion period		5		5	2, 4	

1971 Ratio	Case					
	1	2	3	4	5	6
Sample size	142	542	66	348	50	85
Change NLB		4		2		
CFFO						
NPC − CFFI	2, 4	1, 3	2	1		
Fraser	2, 3, 5	1, 3, 4, 5, 6	1, 2, 4	2, 3, 5, 6	1, 2, 4, 6	2, 4
WCR/S − $m \times (1 - d)$	5	3, 5, 6	2, 4	3, 5, 6	1, 2, 4	2, 4
Short-term debt/total liability	4, 5, 6	4, 5, 6	5, 6	1, 2, 5, 6	1, 2, 3, 4	1, 2, 3, 4
Current ratio	4, 6	4	4	1, 2, 3		1
Cash interval			4, 6	3		3
TL/NW						
ROA		3, 4, 5, 6		2, 6	2	2, 4
Cash conversion period	3	3	1, 2, 4	3		

that within the entire group of ratios, there was a statistically significant difference among the mean values of the liquidity measures based on groupings by case identification. Table 5A-1 shows which cases are significantly different for the group of liquidity measures tested. Clearly, categorizing liquidity by the changes in the net liquid balance and its components helps identify major differences among the values of the liquidity measures used in the test.

Chapter 6

Case Studies

Chapter 5 developed a framework through which an organized analysis of a company's liquidity position can be conducted. It showed how the mean value of several liquidity measures compared for a large sample of industrial firms. This chapter provides case studies of four companies using those liquidity measures. W.T. Grant was chosen because it has become a classic study of liquidity analysis. Chrysler Corporation, one of the great "comebacks" of all times, shows how the liquidity measures behaved over time as Chrysler neared bankruptcy and then rebounded with record profits. John Deere and Company is clearly in a position between insolvency and prosperity. Liquidity analysis of Deere, a company in the farm machinery market that hit bottom in the early 1980s and has yet to recover, provides a good contrast between W.T. Grant and Chrysler. The fourth company, Phillips Petroleum Company, shows how a financial restructuring provoked by corporate raiders can affect the liquidity and financial flexibility position of a company.

W.T. GRANT: A CLASSIC STUDY OF ILLIQUIDITY

The bankruptcy of W.T. Grant in 1975 caught most people by surprise. Although the company had some problems, as indicated by traditional ratios, they did not seem serious enough to cause bankruptcy. As shown by the traditional ratios at the top of Table 6-1, until 1974 W.T. Grant had a relatively slow turnover of receivables and inventory, a moderately low current ratio, increasing leverage, but a healthy level of profitability.

An autopsy, based on analysis of operating cash flow, performed a few years after its bankruptcy revealed a very different picture. The analysis indicated that W.T. Grant had been operating with a negative cash flow from operations for approximately 8 out of the last 10 years of its exis-

TABLE 6-1. Traditional Financial Ratios for W.T. Grant
(dollars in thousands)

	1972	1973	1974
Liquidity ratios			
Current ratio	1.75	1.55	1.60
Quick ratio	1.11	0.91	0.93
Activity ratios			
AR turnover	2.89	3.04	3.10
Inventory turnover	3.12	2.82	2.85
Payables turnover	9.84	14.28	17.61
Working capital position			
Net working capital	$355,674	$346,809	$412,622
Working capital requirements	$543,564	$705,899	$819,767
Net liquid balance	−$187,890	−$359,090	−$407,145
Profitability ratios			
Gross profit margin	32.4%	31.7%	30.8%
Operating profit margin	5.3%	4.8%	2.8%
Net profit margin	2.6%	2.3%	0.5%
ROA	3.7%	3.4%	0.7%
ROE	10.8%	11.3%	2.6%
Leverage ratios			
Times interest earned	4.75	4.01	1.18
Total debt to equity	1.90	2.32	2.87
Growth rates			
Sales growth rate		19.6%	12.5%
Sustainable growth rate	4.5%	5.2%	−3.8%

tence. What that means is that W.T. Grant's operations was a net user of cash each day its doors were open. The only way the company was able to repay its debt principal, interest, dividends, and taxes was to continue to borrow more funds than it was required to disburse.

Traditional Ratio Analysis

Table 6-1 contains many of the traditional financial ratios discussed in Chapters 2 and 4. To begin the analysis, observe the sales growth rate. Sales grew 20 percent in 1973 and another 12 percent in 1974. Grant's sustainable growth rate for those years was 5 and −4 percent, respectively. This excess rate of growth put a severe strain on Grant's ability to finance its operations given its financial and operating structure.

The ratios indicate that Grant was experiencing some problems. For example, the times interest earned ratio fell slightly in 1973 and then dropped significantly in 1974. Its debt-to-equity ratio rose significantly in 1973 and then rose again in 1974.

Although Grant's operating profit margin declined slightly over the period studied, it seemed adequate. The company's net profit margin, ROA, and ROE declined significantly in 1974 primarily due to expenses related to servicing its increasing debt.

Grant's liquidity position as reported by the current and quick ratio seemed reasonable. Its turnover of receivables and inventory, however, seemed ridiculously slow for a department store chain. This slow turnover of receivables and inventory was also reflected in the increasing level of Grant's net working capital and working capital requirements. The growth in working capital requirements exceeded the growth in sales. This trend simply put an additional financial burden on the firm, which was reflected in the trend of the net liquid balance. Grant's net liquid balance was negative, and the liquidity deficit was increasing.

Although the company was not a picture of financial health, the ratios did not seem to indicate its imminent bankruptcy. Without hindsight, the ratios analyzed thus far would indicate a firm that experienced one bad year—1974. Certainly, a firm the size of W.T. Grant can survive one bad year.

Liquidity Analysis

Table 6-2 provides the results of the liquidity measures for W.T. Grant as developed in Chapter 5. Note that the net liquid balance was in a deficit position for each of the 3 years. Just as serious, perhaps, was the fact that the liquidity deficit was worsening. The change in the net liquid balance was composed of two elements, cash flow from operations and the difference between additions to permanent capital and cash flow from investing activities. In 1973, the net liquid balance fell as a result of a negative operating cash flow and an excess of capital expenditures over new permanent capital. In essence, Grant was financing its capital expenditures with short-term funds. A worsening net liquid balance position can be observed in 1974. Even though Grant was able to fund its capital expenditures with an excess of new permanent capital, the negative operating cash flow absorbed the excess capital and forced Grant to rely again on short-term funding. This analysis reveals that Grant's liquidity position can be classified as case 6 in 1973 and case 5 in 1974.

Now review the four cash flow measures in Table 6-2. Grant's cash flow from operations used $116 million in 1973 and another $96.8 million in 1974. Its investing activities required $23.6 and $25.3 million of funds in 1973 and 1974, respectively. Grant was able to secure from its financing activities $120.7 and $137 million in 1973 and 1974, respectively. Together these activities resulted in a reduction in the cash

TABLE 6-2.   Liquidity Measures for W.T. Grant (dollars in thousands)

	1972	1973	1974
NLB decomposition analysis			
Change in NLB		−$171,200	−$ 48,055
CFFO		−$116,084	−$ 96,847
NPC − CFFI		−$ 55,116	$ 48,792
Dollar cash flow figures			
CFFO		−$116,084	−$ 96,847
CFFI		−$ 23,606	−$ 25,341
CFFF		$120,783	$137,196
Change in cash and cash equivalents		−$ 18,907	$ 15,008
Cash conversion period (days)	204	221	222
Sorter–Benston			
Basic defensive interval (days)	144.41	130.98	128.47
Cash interval (days)	13.66	7.06	9.16
Gombola and Ketz			
CFFO/equity		−34.72%	−29.92%
CFFO/sales		− 7.04%	− 5.22%
CFFO/total assets		−10.45%	− 7.73%
CFFO/total debt		−14.95%	−10.42%
WCR/sales	39.44%	42.82%	44.22%
$(WCR/S) - [m \times (1-d)]$	38.42%	41.81%	44.91%
Fraser		−0.0615	−0.0286
Gale and Branch		0.1427	3.6346

and cash equivalents balance of $18.9 million in 1973 and an increase of $15 million in cash and equivalents in 1974. Based on this analysis, it becomes obvious that the increase in cash and equivalents in 1974 was a direct result of borrowing more than was required.

The analysis of Grant's cash flows seems to indicate why the company declared bankruptcy. In 1975, the financial markets simply refused to roll over maturing debt and grant new credit.

Sorter and Benston's interval ratios are also reported in Table 6-2. The basic defensive interval is the ratio of cash, marketable securities, and receivables to daily costs of operations adjusted for noncash charges. Grant had 144 days of expenses covered by its defensive assets; this coverage dropped to 128 days by 1974. Grant's defensive assets appear to provide a more than ample cushion. Most of this cushion, however, was provided by its receivables, which were turning very slowly. Perhaps, in Grant's case, the cash interval is a better measure. This ratio is the same as the basic defensive interval except that receivables are omitted from the numerator. In 1972 the cash interval was 13 days; it declined to

9 days by 1974. This interval measure is probably a more accurate reflection of Grant's liquidity position, which can be interpreted, based on the cash interval, as being very thin. By 1974, Grant only had 9 days of expenses covered by its most liquid assets.

One weakness of the interval measures is that the underlying view of the payment process of corporations is not correct. Corporations cover cash disbursements with cash receipts, not from a pool of liquid assets. A liquidity ratio that takes this into account was developed by Fraser (1983). Its numerator has beginning period cash and cash equivalents plus cash flow from operations for the current period and its denominator consists of beginning period current liabilities. The greater this ratio, the more liquid a corporation. As reported in Table 6-2, the Fraser ratio was negative, indicating that Grant was generating negative operating cash flow that exceeded its level of liquid assets.

Table 6-2 also reports values for the four liquidity ratios used by Gombola and Ketz (1983). The negative signs show that Grant was experiencing severe problems. For example, the CFFO/sales ratio indicates that Grant's sales generated a negative cash flow from operations of −7 percent of sales in 1973 and −5 percent in 1974. Although the trends of these ratios were improving from 1973 to 1974, the negative values should raise grave concerns.

Finally, the working capital to sales ratio indicated that working capital requirements (receivables, inventory, and prepaids minus payables and accruals) were 39 percent in 1972 and increased to 44 percent in 1974. Given the level of technology and managerial efficiency, the level of sales is the single most important influence on the firm's dollar amount of working capital requirements. When WCR is positive, increased sales will require additional investment in the firm's working capital requirements. When WCR is negative, increased sales will generate additional supplies of funds. Note in Table 6-2 that the WCR to sales ratio was positive and rather significant in size. Any sales increase would have required Grant to invest additional funds in its working capital. The results of this analysis would indicate that W.T. Grant's management of its working capital requirements resulted in a relatively illiquid position. Given the working capital to sales relationship, the profitability and dividend policy of the firm could provide an offset to financial pressure created by the working capital cycle. As indicated by the trend in the working capital pressure ratio, however, Grant's profitability and dividend policy actually accentuated the problem. The working capital pressure ratio actually exceeded the working capital requirements to sales ratio in 1974. This is due to Grant's maintenance of its dividend payment in the face of a declining net profit margin.

CHRYSLER: THE EIGHTH WONDER OF THE WORLD

If there were to be an eighth wonder of the world, the turnaround of Chrysler would certainly be in the running. At the end of the 1970s, Chrysler was all but finished. The company was debt ridden, had substantial cash deficits, and was all but ignored by the consuming public. It took a miracle to turn the company around, and that is exactly what happened.

Traditional Ratio Analysis

Chapter 2 provided a financial analysis of Chrysler using traditional ratio analysis. Table 6-3 shows a selection of those ratios from a historical standpoint from 1980 through 1985. The reader may wish to review the ratios in Chapter 2 before continuing.

The trend in the ratios in Table 6-3 is of particular interest. Chrysler was experiencing significant losses as represented by all of its profitability ratios. The year 1981 was the first one of improvement, with the company reporting a positive gross profit margin. After 1980, all the ratios began to show signs of improvement, with the company generating a significant net liquid balance of more than $2.5 billion by 1985. In a sense, Chrysler became a money machine with the ability to repay its debt obligations to the government by 1983.

Liquidity Analysis

To understand Chrysler's liquidity position better, observe its sales growth rate as reported in Table 6-3. Even though Chrysler's sales grew at a rapid pace, the actual growth rate was below Chrysler's sustainable growth rate for every year except 1981.

Table 6-4 displays a decomposition of Chrysler's net liquid balance. This balance was running at a substantial surplus and increased each year except for 1983. Although maintaining a significantly positive balance, the net liquid balance dropped as a result of a substantial capital expansion plan and the significant reduction in long-term debt. The capital expansion program exceeded the acquisition of permanent capital by $2.3 billion. In fact, 1983 was the year that Chrysler repaid the government-guaranteed debt, reducing its long-term debt by over $1 billion. $2.2 billion of this was financed by internal cash flow; the remainder was financed by drawing down the firm's net liquid balance. As seen in Table

TABLE 6-3. Traditional Financial Ratios for Chrysler (dollars in millions)

	1980	1981	1982	1983	1984	1985
Liquidity ratios						
Current ratio	0.94	1.08	1.12	0.80	0.97	1.12
Quick ratio	0.26	0.34	0.54	0.39	0.49	0.64
Activity ratios						
AR turnover	17.92	23.22	40.62	45.97	59.35	103.87
Inventory turnover	4.48	5.57	7.60	8.35	9.55	9.38
Payables turnover	7.28	8.72	9.59	6.88	6.68	6.97
Working capital position						
Net working capital	−$168	$182	$257	−$700	−$136	$584
Working capital requirements	−$149	$3	−$54	−$1,353	−$1,786	−$1,916
Net liquid balance	−$19	$179	$797	$653	$1,651	$2,501
Profitability ratios						
Gross profit margin	−0.6%	10.6%	14.5%	18.9%	21.2%	19.0%
Operating profit margin	−17.2%	−2.8%	0.9%	7.5%	12.1%	10.4%
Net profit margin	−20.0%	−4.8%	1.7%	5.2%	12.1%	7.6%
ROA	−25.8%	−7.6%	2.7%	10.4%	26.3%	13.0%
ROE	−372.3%	−61.0%	17.2%	51.4%	72.0%	38.8%
Leverage ratios						
Times interest earned	−4.05	−0.37	1.58	6.27	26.11	14.19
Total debt to equity	13.41	7.04	5.32	3.96	1.74	1.99
Growth rates						
Sales growth rate	−78.8%	16.9%	0.9%	32.9%	47.3%	9.3%
Sustainable growth rate		−37.8%	21.0%	149.6%	215.9%	56.4%

TABLE 6-4. Liquidity Measures for Chrysler (Dollars in millions)

	1980	1981	1982	1983	1984	1985
NLB decomposition analysis						
Change in NLB		$198	$618	-$ 144	$ 998	$ 850
CFFO		-$260	$864	$2,203	$2,550	$2,136
NPC − CFFI		$458	-$246	-$2,347	-$1,552	-$1,286
Dollar cash flow figures						
CFFO		-$260	$846	$2,203	$2,550	$2,136
CFFI		-$283	-$419	-$ 406	-$ 735	-$2,685
CFFF		$650	$ 49	-$1,624	-$1,184	$1,647
Change in cash and cash equivalents		$107	$493	$ 172	$631	$1,097
Cash conversion period (days)	51	39	19	−1	−10	−10
Sorter–Benston						
Basic defensive interval (days)	29.18	30.44	44.15	40.61	44.20	56.42
No credit interval (days)	−85.09	−57.85	−37.30	−62.48	−45.31	−32.37
Cash interval (days)	11.21	14.76	34.59	31.92	36.97	52.52
Gombola and Ketz						
CFFO/equity		−33%	87%	161%	77%	50%
CFFO/sales		−2%	8%	16%	13%	10%
CFFO/total assets		−4%	13%	32%	28%	17%
CFFO/total debt		−4%	16%	40%	44%	25%
WCR/sales	−1.7%	.03%	−5.3%	−10.1%	−9.1%	−8.8%
(WCR/S) − [m × (1 − d)]	18.3%	4.78%	−7.1%	−16.2%	−20.5%	−15.9%
Fraser		0.12	0.67	0.91	1.08	0.94
Gale and Branch		−13.76	0.53	−0.65	0.62	1.45

6-4, Chrysler's capital expenditures exceeded its change in permanent capital every year except for 1981. The company was able to maintain its liquidity, though, because its cash flow position allowed it to improve its equity position while at the same time reduce its debt as evidenced by the declining debt-to-equity ratio.

Now review the four measures from the statement of cash flow reported in Table 6-4. Chrysler's cash flow from operations was negative in 1981 but reversed to significantly positive flows for 1982 through 1985. Its investing activities required cash in all 5 years of analysis, with a significant increase in investment of $2.6 billion in 1985. Chrysler's financing activities provided cash in 1981, 1982, and 1985 but required cash in 1983 and 1984 as Chrysler paid down significant portions of its debt. Chrysler's balance of cash and cash equivalents increased in each of the years analyzed. Its liquidity position was in either a case 2 or case 3 position for most of the years studied. A major exception occurred in 1983 due to the large pay down of its government obligations; it was then classified as case 4.

It is obvious that Chrysler returned to a very solid financial footing. It will, however, be interesting to see the trend of liquidity indices reported in Table 6-4 from 1980 through 1985. First, an analysis of the Sorter and Benston interval ratios shows that according to the basic defensive interval and the cash interval, Chrysler improved its liquidity position significantly from 1980 to 1985. By 1985, it had 52 days of operating expenses covered by its most liquid assets.

Turning to the Fraser liquidity measure, its value increased from 0.12 to 1.08 in 1984 and then fell to 0.94 in 1985. Chrysler's beginning liquid assets plus its operating cash flow essentially covered its current liabilities.

The Gombola and Ketz liquidity measures indicate that Chrysler was in a very precarious position in 1981, but the position improved substantially during the next 4 years. In fact, from 1982 to 1984, Chrysler's operating cash flow was a healthy percentage of its equity.

Finally, in comparison to the rather large and increasing WCR/sales ratio for W.T. Grant, Chrysler's ratio is not only small but negative. For a manufacturing firm, this is a tremendous liquid position in which to be and is part of the explanation for the significant operating cash flows that Chrysler was able to generate during most of the 1980s. Chrysler's profitability and dividend policy only improve the situation as evidenced by the working capital pressure ratio. Another indicator of this aspect of liquidity is the cash conversion period. Notice how Chrysler's dropped from 51 days in 1980 to a negative 10 days by 1985.

DEERE: HOW LONG CAN IT KEEP RUNNING?

Deere represents a company between the Chrysler turnaround and the Grant bankruptcy. It has been hit hard by the deterioration in market demand for its product, a situation caused primarily by the virtual depression in the farm belt economy. There are, however, signs that the company's management took strong measures to reposition it. The following analysis will apply the financial analysis tools developed in this book to determine the financial and liquidity condition of Deere.

Traditional Ratio Analysis

Table 6-5 presents the traditional financial ratios for Deere. First notice the growth rates from 1980 to 1985. In all except 1984, sales changed at a yearly rate less than the sustainable growth rate. Given this sporadic change in sales, it is somewhat amazing that the company's financial ratios maintained a rather constant pattern. For example, the traditional liquidity measures of the current and quick ratios both grew rather steadily from 1980 to 1985. The current ratio experienced a small dip in 1984.

Deere experienced a steadily deteriorating receivables turnover, dropping from 2.34 in 1980 to 1.40 in 1985. This trend primarily reflects the slump and virtual depression existing in the agriculture market during that time. One bright spot is the control Deere exercised over its inventory. That alone could be crucial in its ability to weather the economic storm.

The company's net working capital position is significantly positive primarily because of the excessive receivables the company was carrying. Its net liquid balance was negative, and the level of the deficit had no clear trend over the period reported.

An ominous trend appeared in Deere's gross profit margin. The ratio slipped from 20.6 percent in 1980 to 17.4 percent in 1985. The remaining profitability measures were very marginal.

Deere's debt-to-equity ratio remained constant. That level of leverage, however, was excessive, as evidenced by the low times interest earned ratio.

Liquidity Analysis

Table 6-6 provides the liquidity measures for Deere from 1980 to 1985. First note the decomposition of the change in Deere's net liquid balance.

TABLE 6-5. Traditional Ratio Measures for Deere (millions of dollars)

	1980	1981	1982	1983	1984	1985
Liquidity ratios						
Current ratio	1.56	1.55	1.57	1.77	1.66	1.79
Quick ratio	1.15	1.17	1.25	1.37	1.41	1.53
Activity ratios						
AR turnover	2.34	2.09	1.60	1.37	1.42	1.40
Inventory turnover	4.95	4.90	5.02	5.20	6.66	7.50
Payables turnover	3.65	3.24	3.41	2.97	3.20	3.27
Working capital position						
Net working capital	$1,198	$1,260	$1,370	$1,650	$1,456	$1,521
Working capital requirements	$1,799	$1,872	$2,212	$2,315	$2,145	$2,022
Net liquid balance	–$ 601	–$ 612	–$ 842	–$ 665	–$ 689	–$ 501
Profitability ratios						
Gross profit margin	20.6%	21.5%	17.1%	17.1%	18.2%	17.4%
Operating profit margin	7.3%	7.7%	0.7%	–0.2%	1.7%	–0.6%
Net profit margin	4.2%	4.6%	1.1%	0.6%	2.4%	0.8%
ROA	4.4%	4.4%	0.9%	0.4%	1.8%	0.6%
ROE	10.4%	10.0%	2.2%	1.0%	4.6%	1.4%
Leverage ratios						
Times interest earned	2.81	2.60	1.05	0.90	1.29	0.83
Total debt to equity	1.37	1.26	1.43	1.58	1.49	1.42
Growth rates						
Sales growth rate		–0.4%	–15.4%	–18.9%	10.9%	–7.7%
Sustainable growth rate	5.4%	4.9%	–2.6%	–1.2%	1.6%	–1.6%

TABLE 6-6. Liquidity Measures for Deere (millions of dollars)

	1980	1981	1982	1983	1984	1985
NLB decomposition analysis						
Change in NLB		–$ 11	–$230	$177	–$ 25	$188
CFFO		$221	–$309	–$ 88	$170	$100
NPC – CFFI		–$231	$ 79	$265	–$195	$ 88
Dollar cash flow figures						
CFFO		$221	–$310	–$ 88	$170	$100
CFFI		–$270	–$ 14	$100	$ 83	–$ 9
CFFF		–$ 10	$369	–$ 83	–$274	–$ 92
Change in cash and cash equivalents		–$ 59	$ 46	–$ 71	–$ 21	–$ 1
Cash conversion period (days)	128	135	191	210	194	194
Sorter–Benston						
Basic defensive interval (days)	177.38	196.15	252.30	287.76	278.80	278.78
No credit interval (days)	22.97	28.26	51.13	77.76	80.86	96.67
Cash interval (days)	10.08	5.95	10.71	5.52	3.21	3.37
Gombola and Ketz						
CFFO/equity		8.8%	–12.7%	–3.9%	7.4%	4.4%
CFFO/sales		4.1%	–6.7%	–2.2%	3.8%	2.5%
CFFO/total assets		3.9%	–5.2%	–1.5%	3.0%	1.8%
CFFO/total debt		7.0%	–8.9%	–2.4%	5.0%	3.1%
WCR/sales	32.9%	34.4%	48.0%	58.3%	48.7%	49.8%
(WCR/S) – [m × (1 – d)]	30.8%	32.2%	49.4%	59.0%	47.9%	50.7%
Fraser		0.291	–0.007	0.206	0.131	0.197
Gale and Branch		0.950	0.724	1.038	–0.627	0.934

Its capital expenditures exceeded its additions of permanent capital for 2 of the 5 years analyzed. The difference was funded in part by the positive cash flow from operations and in part by a reduction of its net liquid balance. Deere's positive cash flow may be hard to understand given its poor profit position and declining receivables turnover. But its ability to generate a positive cash flow is partially explained by the declining level of sales and the control exercised over its inventory.

Deere's cash flow position was somewhat erratic over the period studied. Its operating cash flow was positive except for 1982 and 1983. The level of cash flow from operations, however, fell from 1981 to 1985. Cash flows required from Deere's investing activities were somewhat erratic but were a net provider of funds in 1983 and 1984. Deere's financing activities generally required cash except for 1982.

Deere's cash cycle was obviously at the root of its cash flow problem. The cash conversion period, according to Table 6-6, expanded from 128 days in 1980 to 210 days by 1983 and then subsided to 194 days in 1984 and 1985. The expansion and then minor receding of the cash conversion period was consistent with the trend in the debt-to-equity ratio reported in Table 6-5. Deere responded to the illiquid cash cycle by financing it with increasing amounts of long-term debt.

The first liquidity ratio reported in Table 6-6 for Deere, the Sorter and Benston interval measures, gives conflicting signals, similar to the W.T. Grant situation. The basic defensive interval was quite large and generally increased, a healthy sign. The cash interval, however, was quite small and generally decreased. Given Deere's poor receivables turnover, the cash interval was probably a better liquidity measure. By 1985, Deere had only 3 days of expenses covered by cash and cash equivalents.

The Fraser ratio, excluding 1983, ranged from a low of 0.13 in 1984 to a high of 0.29 in 1981. There was no clear trend. Only about 20 percent of Deere's current liabilities were covered by its beginning cash resources and the intraperiod cash flow. This would seem to indicate a rather low level of liquidity and that Deere had to depend on rolling over its short-term obligations.

The liquidity ratios developed by Gombola and Ketz generally fell in value from 1981 to 1985, a sign of weak liquidity.

The final ratios to be analyzed are the WCR/sales ratio and the working capital pressure ratio. As in the W.T. Grant case, WCR/sales ratio would seem to indicate a relatively illiquid working capital position. Although there was some improvement since 1983, Deere's working capital requirements were substantial in relation to its sales level. Deere's profit position and dividend policy only made the situation worse, as demonstrated by a marginally higher working capital pressure ratio.

PHILLIPS 66: AVOIDING A
TAKEOVER ATTEMPT

The time period chosen to study Phillips Petroleum Company is 1981 through 1986. In 1985, Phillips underwent a substantial financial restructuring to defend itself from two different raiders. The restructuring plan resulted in Phillips buying its stock back through an issuance of debt, which substantially increased its leverage position. In addition, Phillips initiated a program to downsize itself. The time period presents ratio values pre- and postrestructuring in order to assess how liquidity was affected.

Traditional Ratio Analysis

Table 6-7 presents the values for some traditional ratios for Phillips. According to the two liquidity ratios, the company's liquidity position remained stable, with some improvement noted by rising current and quick ratios in 1985 and 1986. Apparently, the raider defense resulting in a significant financial restructuring did not cause the firm's liquidity position to deteriorate. The level of net working capital and net liquid balance generally remained positive, with negative balances for both in 1984 and a negative level of net working capital in 1981. The firm's working capital requirements were negative throughout the period, indicating that its working capital cycle was a net provider of funds. This position occurred because of Phillips' use of a captive finance company.

The firm's activity ratios as represented by the receivables turn, inventory turn, and payables turn remained at a constant level with some year-to-year variation around that level. 1985 and 1986 can be characterized by a slight slowing in receivables turn and payables turn to a level somewhat below the average for the period.

Operating profitability remained stable up to 1986, when the operating profit margin dropped significantly. The net profit margin, however, dropped significantly in 1985 due to the increase in interest expense.

The impact of leverage can readily be seen in the firm's times interest earned ratio and the ratio of total debt to equity. Times interest earned dropped to 7.66 in 1984, dropped again to 3.1 in 1985, then dropped again to 2.0 in 1986. The combination of reduced operating profitability in 1986 and the significant leverage severely strained the firm's finances. The debt-to-equity ratio jumped from an already elevated level of 1.55 in 1984 to 6.16 in 1985.

TABLE 6-7. Traditional Ratio Measures for Phillips (millions of dollars)

	1981	1982	1983	1984	1985	1986
Liquidity ratios						
Current ratio	0.94	1.07	1.01	0.86	1.01	1.26
Quick ratio	0.62	0.74	0.74	0.67	0.75	0.98
Activity ratios						
AR turnover	14.47	12.95	12.64	9.38	9.60	9.57
Inventory turnover	10.22	12.02	13.26	10.40	14.08	10.48
Payables turnover	6.56	7.27	6.88	5.40	6.79	5.79
Working capital position						
Net working capital	−$189	$197	$ 22	−$743	$ 34	$569
Working capital requirements	−$528	−$403	−$742	−$665	−$405	−$384
Net liquid balance	$339	$600	$764	−$ 78	$439	$953
Profitability ratios						
Gross profit margin	44.6%	42.6%	42.5%	42.5%	42.8%	46.9%
Operating profit margin	21.6%	17.6%	19.3%	18.0%	19.1%	12.1%
Net profit margin	5.4%	4.1%	4.7%	5.1%	2.6%	2.3%
ROA	7.8%	5.3%	5.5%	4.8%	3.0%	1.8%
ROE	16.0%	11.1%	11.7%	12.2%	21.3%	11.3%
Leverage ratios						
Times interest earned	14.22	10.29	10.22	7.66	3.10	2.00
Total debt to equity	1.05	1.08	1.12	1.55	6.16	5.14
Growth rates						
Sales growth rate		−2.4%	−3.0%	2.2%	.3%	−36.6%
Sustainable growth rate	11.0%	5.6%	6.6%	7.2%	−6.5%	2.3%

Liquidity Analysis

Several liquidity measures for Phillips are presented in Table 6-8. As can be seen, the company's cash flow position appeared relatively strong. Net liquid balance decomposition analysis indicated that Phillips could be classified as a case 2 firm for all periods studied except 1984. In that year, the net liquid balance declined, resulting in a case 4 classification. Both of those classifications, however, indicated a relatively liquid and viable organization. One troublesome sign was the continual decline in the level of cash flow from operations. This can partially be explained by the downsizing Phillips was experiencing due to its restructuring. But the fact remains that operating cash flow in 1986 was roughly half its 1983 level.

Analysis of the various cash flow categories is also revealing. Cash flow from investing activities represented an outflow of funds through 1984. After that time CFFI represented a net inflow of funds primarily from the liquidation of assets resulting from the firm's restructuring activities. In 1985 and 1986 cash flow from financing activities actually used funds due to a substantial stock buy-back and a 200 percent stock dividend along with a significant increase in dividends paid. These activities more than offset the funds obtained through the issuance of debt and preferred stock. 1986 witnessed Phillips paying down its enormous debt obligation.

A major factor explaining Phillips' ability to sustain its enormous debt load was its strong working capital cycle. Note that the cash conversion period was extremely low generally, running less than 10 days. This extreme position resulted from the purchase of receivables by Phillips Petroleum Credit Corporation. Because of that, the WCR/S ratio and the working capital pressure ratio both were negative, indicating that the firm's working capital cycle provided, rather than used, funds.

The Sorter–Benston interval measures were erratic. For example, the cash interval ranged from a low of 17.2 days in 1985 to a high of 49.3 days in 1984. No clear trend existed.

The Gombola and Ketz cash flow ratios pointed to an ominous trend that developed, with most of their ratios steadily declining from their peaks in 1983. An example is the cash flow to total debt ratio, which fell from 35.6 percent in 1983 to 11.2 percent in 1986. Clearly, the slowing of cash flow from operations and the significant increase in debt affected the firm's financial flexibility.

Finally, the Fraser ratio dropped significantly in 1984 due somewhat to a slightly lower operating cash flow level but primarily to a drastic increase in current liabilities.

TABLE 6-8. Liquidity Measures for Phillips (millions of dollars)

	1981	1982	1983	1984	1985	1986
NLB decomposition analysis						
Change in NLB		$ 261	$ 164	-$ 842	$ 517	$ 514
CFFO		$1,826	$2,459	$2,293	$1,846	$1,159
NPC – CFFI		-$1,565	-$2,295	-$3,135	-$1,329	-$ 645
Dollar cash flow figures						
CFFO		$1,826	$2,459	$2,293	$1,846	$1,159
CFFI		-$2,149	-$2,030	-$3,499	$ 4	$ 362
CFFF		$ 221	-$ 316	$2,194	-$3,068	-$1,056
Change in cash and cash equivalents		-$ 102	$ 113	$ 988	-$1,218	$ 465
Cash conversion period (days)	5	8	3	6	10	10
Sorter–Benston						
Basic defensive interval (days)	49.87	50.69	54.97	92.92	59.09	91.86
No credit interval (days)	-30.00	-17.36	-19.56	-46.12	-20.09	-1.85
Cash interval (days)	22.08	19.90	23.44	49.27	17.21	47.92
Gombola and Ketz						
CFFO/equity		31.4%	39.7%	34.4%	94.1%	57.4%
CFFO/sales		11.5%	15.9%	14.6%	11.7%	11.6%
CFFO/total assets		15.1%	18.8%	13.5%	13.1%	9.4%
CFFO/total debt		29.0%	35.6%	22.3%	15.3%	11.2%
WCR/sales	-3.2%	-2.5%	-4.8%	-4.2%	-2.6%	-3.8%
(WCR/S) – [$m \times (1 - d)$]	-6.6%	-4.5%	-7.3%	-7.1%	-1.7%	-4.3%
Fraser		1.003	1.128	0.598	1.203	0.822
Gale and Branch		1.244	1.095	0.922	0.558	-0.248

SUMMARY

Liquidity measures provide new insight into understanding the liquidity position of firms and clearly supplement the traditional ratios generally used in financial analysis. Liquidity analysis includes assessment of the operating cash flow position of a firm and analysis of the investing and financing cash flows.

REFERENCES

Fraser, Lyn M. 1983. Cash flow from operations and liquidity analysis: A new financial ratio for commercial lending decisions. *The Journal of Commercial Bank Lending* 66(3):45–52.

Gombola, Michael J., and J. Edward Ketz. 1983. A note on cash flow and classification patterns of financial ratios. *The Accounting Review* 58(1):105–114.

Sorter, G. H., and George Benston. 1960. Appraising the defensive position of a firm: The interval measure. *The Accounting Review* 35:633–640.

Chapter 7

Special Topics

This chapter completes the discussion of liquidity analysis by considering four special topics: how cash flow analysis can be used to predict bankruptcy, how growth and inflation affect the liquidity position of a firm, how cash flow analysis can help assess the quality of earnings, and the need for small business owners to pay particular attention to cash flow.

PREDICTING BANKRUPTCY

Many analysts have attempted to develop a model that could accurately predict the bankruptcy of firms. Chen and Shimerda (1981) noted that studies found 34 different ratios helpful in predicting bankruptcy. The studies, however, are inconsistent in suggesting which ratios are most useful, and it is possible that the sample of ratios from any one analysis is only relevant for firms with similar financial and operating characteristics as the firms tested in the study. Also, many of the 34 ratios are similar or highly correlated to one another. To overcome this redundancy, Chen and Shimerda classified all but the following 10 of the ratios into one of the seven categories suggested by Pinches, Mingo, and Caruthers (1973):

- Quick assets/inventory
- Net income/common equity
- Quick flow $= \dfrac{\text{Cash} + \text{marketable securities} + \text{average monthly sales}}{(\text{COGS} - \text{depreciation} + \text{selling and administrative expenses})/12}$
- Funds flow/current liabilities
- Net income/sales
- Funds flow/total debt

- Working capital/total assets
- Long-term debt/current assets
- No-credit interval = $\dfrac{\text{quick assets} - \text{current liabilities}}{\text{operating expenses} - \text{depreciation}}$
- Retained earnings/total assets

The seven categories classify ratios according to their common information. In addition, each ratio has unique information. The key is to choose a set of ratios that "capture most of the common information contained in their factors, and as a group, contain more of the unique information than any other set of ratios" (Chen and Shimerda 1981, p. 59). Choosing too many highly correlated ratios or several ratios from the same factor could produce sample-sensitive, distorted results. Some of the studies incorporated a cash flow type of measure but generally resorted to net income plus depreciation.

Zeta Model

In 1977, Altman, Haldeman, and Narayanan released a paper that presented the zeta model for bankruptcy prediction. The accuracy of the model was 96 percent 1 year before bankruptcy and 70 percent 5 years before bankruptcy. The following seven variables were used in the zeta model:

$X1$ = EBIT/total assets

$X2$ = Stability of earnings measured by standard error of a 10-year trend

$X3$ = EBIT/total interest payments (including the amount imputed from the capitalized lease liability)

$X4$ = Retained earnings/total assets

$X5$ = Current ratio (found to be more effective than other liquidity ratios)

$X6$ = Common equity/total capital (market value rather than book value is used)

$X7$ = Size as measured by total assets using a log transformation

Consideration of Economic Environment in Bankruptcy Prediction

Although many studies such as that of Altman et al. have been completed, Mensah (1984) criticizes such bankruptcy prediction models that use multiple discriminant analysis but fail to recognize the underlying economic conditions at the time of the study. He contends that economic conditions could be a contributing factor to the inconsistent results of the different models. The bankruptcy models, for example, identify common attributes of faltering companies, but they fail to identify the external economic factors that either make the company's difficulties more severe or eventually lead to the company's downfall. The tests are usually conducted using pooled data across different time periods without proper consideration of the variety of economic conditions occurring during those periods. Mensah cites inflation, interest rates, credit availability, and business cycle position as the crucial economic factors to consider.

Also, different industries may require different prediction models. In an expansionary economy, the accuracy prediction rate was 85 percent for manufacturing firms and 75 percent for retail firms. In a recessionary environment, the rate was 88 percent for manufacturing firms and 63.5 percent for retailing firms (Mensah 1984, p. 393).

Cash Flow Variables and Bankruptcy Prediction

Casey and Bartczak (1984, 1985) presented the results of a study that suggested that cash flow form operations is not a useful predictor of financial failure. In the last several years, accountants and financial analysts have regarded cash flow information as crucial to assessing the financial health of businesses. More and more, in the shadow of the W.T. Grant bankruptcy, executives seem to prefer evaluating a firm's liquidity on a cash rather than a working capital basis. Casey and Bartczak warn, however, that cash flow information is not a panacea for evaluating the financial strength of a firm. They suggest, for example, that strong cash flows can result when a declining firm chooses not to reinvest its cash resources, and weak cash flows can be overcome by a growth company that has the ability to restructure or refinance its debt temporarily until it reaches a more stable position. In both situations, the cash flow position does not tell the whole story about the financial strength of a firm.

In the Casey and Bartczak study, CFFO was computed using the indirect method. First, accounting net income was adjusted for noncash flow revenues and expenses (including depreciation) to determine working capital from operations. Working capital from operations was then adjusted for short-term accruals such as accounts receivable, inventories, and accounts payable to yield CFFO.

Casey and Bartczak studied 60 bankrupt and 230 nonbankrupt firms from 1971 to 1982. The three variables CFFO, CFFO/current liabilities (CL), and CFFO/total liabilities (TL) were used as the potential bankruptcy predictors. The results showed that CFFO, CL, and TL could only predict bankruptcy 60, 75, and 72 percent of the time, respectively, 1 year before failure. These percentages declined dramatically for time periods more than 1 year before bankruptcy.

The CFFO ratios were also shown to be less accurate than the following traditional set of ratios: net income/total assets, cash/total assets, current assets/current liabilities, net sales/current assets, current assets/total assets, and total liabilities/owners' equity. These traditional ratios had an overall accuracy rate of 86 percent.

Furthermore, combining the CFFO ratios with the traditional ratios did not significantly improve the prediction results. According to Casey and Bartczak, the CFFO ratios do not even contain marginal value, and "other factors such as a company's debt level, its access to the debt and equity markets, the salability of its capital assets, and its reservoir of liquid assets may be better indicators of survival prospects than cash flow data" (Casey and Bartczak 1984, p. 65).

Countering Casey and Bartczak's argument, Gentry, Newbold, and Whitford (1985a, 1985b) concluded from their analysis that cash flow information can be helpful in predicting bankruptcy. The Gentry, Newbold, and Whitford (GNW) model breaks funds flow information into the following components:

- Operations
- Working capital (broken down further as receivables, inventory, other assets, payables, other current liabilities)
- Financial
- Fixed coverage expenses or interest and lease payments
- Capital expenditures
- Dividends
- Other assets and liability flows
- Change in cash and marketable securities

GNW distinguished their study from the Casey and Bartczak study by using a broader base of cash flow components that use complete financial information from the balance sheet and income statement as opposed to only operating cash flow. The GNW model also incorporated the changes in cash that result from factors such as interest and lease payments, capital expenditures, and dividends. Contrast this with the Casey and Bartczak model that confined its analysis to cash flow from operations and ignores the other components of funds flow. Indeed, they even stated that these other factors are probably critical to the bankruptcy event.

The GNW model is not a superior predictor just because of the funds flow definition it uses. Rather, it seems to show different results because it links bankruptcy to several individual components of funds flow rather than to a single component cash flow from operations.

The GNW model studied 33 failed companies that either were involved in bankruptcy suits or were liquidated. The failed companies were matched with 33 nonfailed companies on the basis of their industry classification, asset base, and sales size. Twenty-one of the 33 failed companies were industrial and 12 were a mixture.

The model correctly classified 79 percent of the failed companies and 88 percent of the nonfailed companies using data from 1 year before the failure period. The accuracy percentage fell to 79 percent for the nonfailed companies when average figures for 3 years before bankruptcy were introduced.

By breaking their model down even further, GNW discovered a significant difference between failed and nonfailed firms in the percentage of cash outflows used for dividends. Dividends accounted for an average of 9.2 percent of the total outflows for the surviving companies and only 1.8 percent for failed companies. This difference was also significant when a mean of the dividends flows for the 3 years before bankruptcy was used. This suggests that the proportion of a firm's cash outflows used for dividends could be a useful predictor of financial failure.

GNW's study also revealed that 1 year before bankruptcy the failed companies invested a significantly smaller percentage of their funds in plant and equipment than did the nonfailed companies. Furthermore, in the period before failure, the bankrupt companies had a reduction in receivables that increased their cash flows, and the nonfailed companies had an increase in receivables that reduced their cash flows. The investment and receivables funds flow components, however, do not accurately predict financial failure further in advance than 1 year.

The last step of the study showed that when nine traditional ratios were combined with the cash flow components, the increase in the explanatory power was significant at the 5 percent level. By reversing the process, when the cash flow components were combined with the traditional ratios it was significant at the 1 percent level. Although both sets of measures provide additional discriminating information when they are combined, it appears as though the cash flow measures provide a slightly more significant impact. The following traditional ratios were used:

- Net income/total assets
- EBIT/total assets

- Total debt/total assets
- Cash flow/total debt
- Net working capital/total assets
- Current assets/current liabilities
- Cash plus marketable securities/current liabilities
- Natural log of total assets
- Market value of equity/book value of equity

These findings seem to counter Casey and Bartczak's argument that cash flow information does not have at least "marginal value" for bankruptcy prediction models. Furthermore, the GNW model suggests that cash flow information can be used in conjunction with other ratios in improving the accuracy of bankruptcy prediction models.

EFFECTS OF INFLATION AND GROWTH ON LIQUIDITY

Denison (1976, p. 33) notes that sales growth and inflationary pressures lead to "cash leakages" in most businesses. A study by Gale and Branch (1981, p. 132) supports the conclusion that cash flow is lowest when sales are increasing. If sales are growing, a dramatic increase in return on investment is needed just to "breakeven in cash flow." Plant and equipment additions and larger amounts of working capital absorb cash during these rapid growth periods.

Cash flow also decreases when inflation increases. A rise in selling prices does theoretically generate more cash, but this "extra cash" is absorbed by the simultaneous increase in operating costs and amount of money tied up in inventories and accounts receivable. Therefore, cash flow varies inversely with both market sales growth and inflation. One must carefully consider these two sources of cash "leakage" when assessing liquidity.

To better understand the impact that inflation has on liquidity analysis, it is necessary to understand the impact that inflation has on accounting statements, the basic source of information for analyzing liquidity. Many forces cause the dollar values of accounts on financial statements to change. The dollar balance of accounts receivable may change, for example, because the volume of credit sales increase, credit-granting standards are relaxed, or inflation increased the dollar value of a given sales volume. In general, the dollar value of all working capital accounts, including receivables, inventory, and payables can change for three reasons: a change in business volume, productivity changes, or inflation effects. Since financial reporting is based on historical costs, it is important to understand how to adjust financial statements during periods of changing price levels.

To begin, all balance sheet accounts must be classified as either monetary or nonmonetary. Accounts are considered monetary if they are paid by currency. Monetary accounts require no price level adjustment. Nonmonetary accounts must be adjusted to account for price level changes. In general, cash, marketable securities, and receivables are monetary assets, whereas inventory, fixed plant, goodwill, and other intangibles are nonmonetary assets. Most liability accounts are considered monetary, whereas equity accounts are considered nonmonetary.

The income statement must be adjusted in two important areas to arrive at a current cost statement. First, cost of goods sold must be adjusted because it is affected by the nonmonetary inventory account. Second, depreciation expense must be adjusted to reflect the impact of price level changes on the replacement value of a firm's stock of plant and equipment.

Changing price levels affect the true value of many items on the balance sheet and income statement. Since all ratios and liquidity measures are computed directly from these statements, interpretation of these indicators must take into account the impact of changing price levels in order to assess the true financial condition of an enterprise.

Based on the above discussion, it is relatively easy to understand how changing price levels can affect liquidity. First, tax liability is computed on historical based income statements, with the exception of inventory adjustments based on last-in first-out (LIFO) or first-in first-out (FIFO). During periods of rising prices, a firm showing an accounting profit on a historical cost based income statement and paying dividends out of this accounting profit may actually be earning a real loss on a current cost basis. Dividends, in such a case, represent a return of capital, not a return on investment. Thus, cash flow is reduced by excessive tax payments in relation to the true replacement cost of assets and excessive dividends based on accounting profits but economic losses. Such an erosion of the capital base can have serious implications for the financial flexibility and liquidity of the enterprise.

ASSESSING THE QUALITY OF EARNINGS

Various cash flow measures can be related to their accrual counterparts to assess the quality of accounting data. Three relatively simple comparisons can be made: the ratio of cash receipts to sales, the ratio of cash expenses to accrual-based expenses on the income statement, and the ratio of cash flow to net income. These ratios for W.T. Grant, Chrysler, and Deere are shown in Table 7-1. The before-tax CFFO and after-tax CFFO are related to those cash flow measures discussed in Chapter 3. The closer these ratios are to 1.00 and the more stable they are, the greater the quality of earnings.

Table 7-1 indicates that the ratio of cash receipts to sales is close to 1.00 for all three companies. Grant's cash expenses exceed its accrual expenses by a few percentage points, whereas the same ratio for Chrysler and Deere is less than 1.00. Grant's before-tax CFFO to operating profit ratio indicates a significant problem, as does its after-tax CFFO less interest and other expenses to net profit ratio. These same two ratios for Chrysler and Deere show a high degree of volatility.

LIQUIDITY AND THE SMALL BUSINESS

Too often analysts and investors rely on the flawed assumption that small businesses are much like bigger businesses, only with lower sales volume, a smaller asset base, and fewer employees. Welsh and White (1981) argue that within the business environment, small size results in a special condition that distinguishes those firms from their larger counterparts. This condition, referred to as resource poverty, requires an entirely different set of management strategies on the part of the owners. The small firm must make the most efficient use of available resources. Anything short of this will result in failure.

The five distinguishing characteristics of small firms that necessitate a special set of operating strategies for the owner/manager are as follows:

1. A small firm is disproportionately located in local markets. Fragmented and highly competitive, these markets are often characterized by price competition in the face of falling profits.

2. Owner's compensation tends to be a proportionately larger share of total revenues.

3. Services commonly used by large firms, such as accounting, legal, and planning, are unavailable or unaffordable for small firms.

4. Employee training programs are underused, resulting in labor inefficiencies.

5. Small firms are more sensitive to the external operating environment. Regulation, changes in the tax codes, and business interruption have proportionately greater impact.

TABLE 7-1. Assessing the Quality of Earnings

W.T. Grant	1973	1974
Operating cash receipts/sales	0.96	0.97
Operating cash expenses/accrual expenses	1.065	1.026
Before-tax CFFO/operating profit	−1.125	−0.964
After-tax CFFO − other expenses − interest/net profit	−3.376	−10.918

Chrysler	1981	1982	1983	1984	1985
Operating cash receipts/sales	1.005	1.018	0.996	0.998	1.006
Operating cash expenses/accrual expenses	0.978	0.925	0.897	0.941	0.981
Before-tax CFFO/operating profit	0.03	11.317	2.210	1.409	1.217
After-tax CFFO − other expenses − interest/net profit	0.383	6.105	3.385	1.443	1.306

Deere	1981	1982	1983	1984	1985
Operating cash receipts/sales	0.949	0.942	0.996	0.955	1.047
Operating cash expenses/accrual expenses	0.922	0.971	0.915	0.917	0.958
Before-tax CFFO/operating profit	1.270	−3.045	−48.30	3.215	−13.54
After-tax CFFO − other expenses − interest/net profit	1.618	−1.199	14.86	1.806	11.10

The problem is that many small business managers do not understand the importance of cash flow and often overlook the important task of liquidity management. Edmunds (1979) cites two reasons that "the discipline of a cash budget" is especially important to small businesses:

1. A cash budget can encourage a business to develop other necessary financial records.
2. A cash budget integrates the effects of operations on both the balance sheet and the income statement.

A cash budget helps the small business manager overcome the tendency to pay too much attention to the income statement. Small businesses often concentrate on reducing fixed costs per unit through growth in sales. The fallacy of this strategy is that few costs are truly fixed. The result is that the improved profitability is too often short lived and achieved only at the "expense" of a cash shortage. This can lead a small business manager to "overexpand operations beyond the capacity of his cash resources" (Edmunds 1979, p. 174).

A cash budget, therefore, helps a manager clearly distinguish between profit and cash flow. The major source of the difference is the fact that few of the payment cycles facing the firm fall into the uniform monthly cycle portrayed by the income statement.

Growth for the sake of growth can lead to expanding beyond an operation's capacity for generating cash. As an enterprise grows, more pressure is placed on the firm through expanding asset requirements. Sales growth automatically generates increased requirements for inventory to support higher sales levels. Higher sales translates into larger accounts receivable balances. As sales capacity is reached, there are increased pressures to expand capital assets, especially in equipment-intensive operations such as manufacturing. Regardless of the market pressures, such capital expansions should not be considered unless the cash flow projections indicate enough cash available to purchase equipment outright or, more likely, service the debt used to finance the purchase.

How does the entrepreneur minimize the likelihood of encountering severe cash flow problems? Edmunds (1979) lists the following steps to monitor cash flow successfully:

1. Using historical data as a basis to make a sales projection.
2. Obtain a cash payments schedule to analyze accounts receivable collection.
3. Estimate total cash inflows; that is, cash sales, accounts receivable payment pattern, and sale of other assets.

4. Test the reasonableness of the inflows by comparing them to the appropriate industry data.
5. Make a budget for all operating and capital expenditures to develop a cash outflow schedule.
6. Establish a priority schedule for cash outflows listing the order in which payments are made, for example, (a) fixed costs, (b) payrolls, (c) operating expenses, and (d) capital items.
7. Pay officer compensation only if there is a net cash balance remaining (do not overdraw cash to pay officers).
8. If there is no cash available, see an accountant or banker about the possibilities of using float, accounts payable, or loans for temporary financing.
9. If credit is needed, go through steps 1 to 7 to see if more cash can be generated by adjusting operating policies (reducing costs or increasing sales). Otherwise the firm may experience a severe cash shortage that could lead to financial failure.

Liquidity management is critically important to small businesses. Even though a small business can survive an amazingly long time without a high level of profitability, it will fail as soon as it cannot meet its cash obligations. For the small firm, cash flow is more important than profit or return on investment. Liquidity means survival and should be the top priority.

Current empirical research often does not support the claim that cash flow has an independent impact on the operations of a firm. Several studies have indicated that profitability and cash flow are actually measuring the same characteristic or aspect of firm performance (Casey and Bartczak 1984, 1985). One of the reasons for this misclassification of financial characteristics is that researchers often overlook the differences between large and small firms discussed here. Empirical differences between large and small firms are developed and discussed below.

Data matrices for 1981 were factor analyzed and produced patterns of financial ratios for different sized firms. Data were obtained from the COMPUSTAT ™ data tapes, where screening resulted in 1475 industrial firms for which 28 financial ratios were calculated.

Table 7-2 presents the classification pattern suggested by the factor analysis. When the sample of firms was divided according to asset size, the pattern varied significantly. For all firms with total assets of less than $1 billion, cash flow from operations formed a separate factor distinct from the return on investment factor. For firms with total assets greater than $1 billion, however, the two merged into one factor.

TABLE 7-2. Classification Pattern for Financial Ratios

1. Cash Flow from Operations 　CFFO/net worth 　CFFO/sales 　CFFO/total assets 　CFFO/total liabilities 　CFFO − dividends	*5. Leverage* 　Current liabilities/net worth 　Total liabilities/net worth 　Fixed assets/net worth
2. Return on Investment 　Operating profit margin 　After-tax profit margin 　ROA 　ROE	*6. Inventory Intensity* 　Cost of sales/inventory 　Current liabilities/inventory
	7. Receivables Intensity 　Sales/receivables
3. Net Liquid Balance 　NLB/total assets 　Δ NLB 　NPC − CFFI	*8. Funds Flexibility* 　CFFI/total funds 　CFFF/total funds
4. Short-Term Liquidity 　Current ratio 　Quick ratio 　Cash/total assets 　NLB/total assets 　Sorter–Benston cash 　　interval	

The results seem to indicate that when cash flow from operations is properly defined for smaller firms (those with assets less than $1 billion), it captures a characteristic of firm performance distinct from that captured by the measures of profitability. Thus, cash and profit are not the same. For large firms (those with total assets greater than $1 billion), however, these two aspects of firm performance are measured by the same factor. For empirical purposes these two sets of ratios are similar.

Table 7-3 presents additional findings regarding the liquidity of firms. It shows the mean values, by asset size, of a sample of financial ratios and liquidity measures during 1981 for the sample of firms analyzed in Chapter 5 from the COMPUSTAT™ database. Note that the sample consists entirely of publicly held companies; the analysis should not be generalized to cover privately held businesses.

Some of the liquidity measures do not show any clear trend when compared by asset size. These include the Fraser ratio, the Sorter–Benston cash interval, and the leverage ratio; that is, total liabilities to net worth. Other ratios, however, do show some interesting trends. The working capital pressure ratio and the cash conversion period, for example, both improve as firms become larger. The larger firms are generally

TABLE 7-3. Mean Value Liquidity Measures by Asset Size for 1981

Total Assets	Millions of Dollars						
	Less Than 10	10 to 25	25 to 50	50 to 100	100 to 500	500 to 1000	More Than 1000
Sample size	32	101	178	193	500	143	328
Change in NLB	−$0.36	$0.21	$0.83	$0.65	$0.27	$2.10	−$ 50.28
CFFO	$0.16	$0.54	$1.45	$3.77	$17.18	$72.65	$394.17
NPC − CFFI	−$0.52	−$0.33	−$0.61	−$3.11	−$16.94	−$70.54	−$444.45
Fraser ratio	0.64	0.64	0.55	0.52	0.65	0.90	0.64
WC pressure	0.27	0.28	0.25	0.23	0.22	0.17	0.17
Short-term debt/Total liabilities	0.25	0.17	0.14	0.12	0.10	0.08	0.10
Current ratio	2.68	2.73	2.69	2.48	2.31	2.02	1.77
Cash interval (days)	33	39	36	23	30	27	23
Total liabilities/Net worth	0.74	1.14	1.32	1.59	1.50	1.26	1.37
ROA (%)	0.74	5.64	4.48	4.62	5.79	7.32	6.11
Cash conversion period (days)	127	153	123	117	115	96	97

more profitable based on return on assets and generally use a smaller proportion of short-term debt. In addition, the current ratio declines from a high of 2.73 for firms in the $10 to $25 million group to 1.77 for the largest firms. One conclusion is that liquidity is improved as firms grow larger because the larger firms rely less heavily on short-term debt, they are generally more profitable, and their working capital cycle exerts less pressure. Although the current ratio is smaller for larger firms, this appears to be caused by an improved working capital cycle, as evidenced by the falling working capital pressure ratio and the falling cash conversion period, rather than a deterioration in liquidity.

Analysis of the net liquid balance position also results in interesting findings. All asset size categories with the exception of the smallest and largest can be classified as case 1 companies (using the NLB classification scheme developed previously). The net liquid balance fell in 1981 for the smallest and largest asset groups because operating cash flow was not large enough to fund the net investment needs of the firms. Thus, firms in these two asset groups must draw down their net liquid balances in order to fund their investments.

SUMMARY

This chapter discussed four topics in which cash flow and liquidity are important dimensions. The first was the importance of cash flow data in predicting bankruptcy. Although cash flow from operations is not an important predicting variable, other cash flow variables seem to contribute to bankruptcy prediction.

The second was the impact that inflation and growth have on liquidity. Both cause leakages in liquidity that can have a detrimental impact on a firm.

The third topic was cash flow measures used to assess the quality of earnings reported on traditional financial statements. The approach was to calculate a cash flow based equivalent of an accrual-based income statement item as a basis for comparison. The more divergent the accrual-based income statement item is from its cash flow equivalent, the lower the quality of earnings.

The final topic was how liquidity varies by asset size. It was found that many liquidity measures vary by the size of a firm. The relative importance of cash flow as a measure distinct from profitability is also affected by the size of a firm. For small firms, cash flow appears to be distinct from profitability. For firms larger than $1 billion in assets, cash flow and profitability appear to be similar.

REFERENCES

Altman, Edward I., Robert G. Haldeman, and P. Narayanan. 1977. Zeta analysis. *Journal of Banking and Finance* 1(1):29–54.

Casey, Cornelius J., and Norman J. Bartczak. 1984. Cash flow—It's not the bottom line. *Harvard Business Review* 62(4):61–65.

―――. 1985. Using operating cash flow data to predict financial distress: Some extensions. *Journal of Accounting Research* 23(1):384–401.

Chen, Kung H., and Thomas A. Shimerda. 1981. An empirical analysis of useful financial ratios. *Financial Management* 10(1):51–59.

Denison, D. R. 1976. The banker's shell game, lending against cash flow. *The Journal of Commercial Bank Lending* 58(9):29–38.

Edmunds, Stahrl W. 1979. Performance measures for small business. *Harvard Business Review* 57(1):172–178.

Gale, Bradley, and Ben Branch. 1981. Cash flow analysis: More important than ever. *Harvard Business Review* 59(4):131–136.

Gentry, James A., Paul Newbold, and David T. Whitford. 1985a. Predicting bankruptcy: If cash flow's not the bottom line, what is? *Financial Analysts Journal* (September/October):47–54.

―――. 1985b. Classifying bankruptcy firms with funds flow components. *Journal of Accounting Research* 23(1):146–160.

Mensah, Yaw M. 1984. An examination of the stationarity of multivariate bankruptcy prediction models: A methodological study. *Journal of Accounting Research* 22(1):380–393.

Pinches, G., K. Mingo, and J. Caruthers. 1973. The stability of financial patterns in industrial organizations. *Journal of Finance* 28(2):389–396.

Welsh, John A., and Jerry F. White. 1981. A small business is not a little big business. *Harvard Business Review* 59(4):18–32.

Chapter 8

Cash Flow Analysis Using the Microcomputer

Microcomputer technology has advanced dramatically in the last decade, allowing users to analyze large amounts of data quickly and efficiently. Since the introduction of the Apple computer in 1978 and the IBM PC in 1981, the desktop computer has become standard equipment both at home and in the office.

It is essential that financial statement users know how to use microcomputers and their software packages. Not only is the convenience of word processing important, but the speed and reliability of electronic spreadsheets are critical to the accurate and efficient processing of financial data.

The planner should become proficient with at least one spreadsheet package, such as Lotus 1-2-3™, SuperCalc™, or Microsoft Multiplan™; the general nature of each is the same. As a worksheet is developed, the user can define relationships among variables and groups of variables, do standard or complicated mathematical operations, and make logical comparisons to determine values in the worksheet.

WORKSHEET TEMPLATE

A main advantage of spreadsheet programs is that when applications such as worksheets, graphs, and databases are used repetitively, a *worksheet template* can be created that will speed data processing and analysis considerably. A template is simply a standardized worksheet with all the relevant titles, formulas, and logic statements designed for a specific application and saved as a separate program.

Extreme care must be taken when creating a template. If not, errors in the analysis can result. In addition, input data must be correctly entered or manipulations will produce errors.

As was mentioned, templates automate processing and thus save time and effort when repetitive analyses are performed on different data sets. Each time an analysis is performed, these steps are involved: (1) loading the spreadsheet package, (2) loading the worksheet template, and (3) loading the relevant data. If a template is appropriately designed, it will calculate all the specified values. Subsequent analysis can then be performed simply by changing some values. An accountant might create a tax template to streamline the tax preparation process. A financial planner might develop an investment template to evaluate the risk/return characteristics of a stock issue.

This chapter develops a worksheet template for generating cash flow statements using both the indirect and direct approach. It uses the functions and terminology of Lotus 1-2-3™, but the principles apply to any spreadsheet software. Begin, therefore, by loading Lotus 1-2-3 (or another spreadsheet program).

The template can be divided into three parts: (1) a data input sheet consisting of an income statement and comparative balance sheet, (2) a cash flow statement using the direct method, and (3) a cash flow statement using the indirect method. A certain familiarity with the spreadsheet software is needed to take full advantage of the following discussion. Users who are unfamiliar with the packages should refer closely to the users' manuals provided with the programs.

Data Input Section

Table 8-1 presents a simplified balance sheet and income statement that will serve as the data input section of the cash flow module. The data input section is located in cells A1 through H65. Enter the labels and formulas as they appear in the table.

To guarantee that data are entered in only the cells in which they are expected, protect the noninput fields. To do so, first invoke the {Worksheet Global Protect Enable} command, /WGPE. Next, unprotect all cells in which data are to be entered by invoking the {Range Unprotect} command, /RU, until all data input fields have been unprotected. When the prompt "Enter range to unprotect" appears, type "A2.A2". Repeat the second step to unprotect all data input fields:

TABLE 8-1. Simplified Balance Sheet and Income Statement

	A^a	B	C	D	E	F^b	G^c	H
1								
2		Company Name						
3		$ DENOMINATION: $ · · · · · ·		Date				
4						Year 1	Year 2	
5		ASSETS						
6		Cash				0	0	
7		Cash equivalents				0	0	
8		Accounts and notes receivable (trade)				0	0	
9		Inventory				0	0	
10		Prepaid expenses				0	0	
11		All other current				0	0	
12								
13		CURRENT ASSETS				@SUM(F6.F11)	@SUM(G6.G11)	
14								
15		Gross fixed assets				0	0	
16		Accumulated depreciation				0	0	
17		Intangibles (net)				0	0	
18		All other noncurrent				0	0	
19								
20		TOTAL ASSETS				+F13+F15−F16 +F17+F18	+G13+G15−G16 +G17+G18	
21								

TABLE 8-1. (*Continued*)

A^a	B	C	D	E	F^b	G^c	H
22	LIABILITIES AND NET WORTH						
23	Accounts and notes payable (trade)				0	0	
24	Notes payable (short term)				0	0	
25	Accruals				0	0	
26	Accrued taxes				0	0	
27	Current Mat long-term debt				0	0	
28	All other current				0	0	
29					@SUM(F23.F28)	@SUM(G23.G28)	
30	CURRENT LIABILITIES						
31					0	0	
32	Long-term debt				0	0	
33	Deferred income tax				0	0	
34	All other noncurrent				0	0	
35	Preferred stock				0	0	
36	Common stock				0	0	
37	Paid-in capital and other				0	0	
38	Treasury stock				0	0	
39	Earned surplus				0	0	
40							
41	TOTAL LIABILITIES AND NET WORTH				@SUM(F30,F32.F37, −F38,F39)	@SUM(G30,G32.G37, −G38,G39)	

		F	G
42			
43	INCOME DATA		
44	Net sales	0	0
45	Other operating income	0	0
46			
47	Total operating revenue	+F44+F45	+G44+G45
48			
49	Cost of sales	0	0
50			
51	Gross profit	+F47−F49	+G47−G49
52			
53	Operating expenses (excluding depreciation)	0	0
54	Lease and rental expense	0	0
55	Depreciation and amortization	0	0
56	Other operating expenses	0	0
57			
58	Operating profit	+F51−@SUM(F53.F56)	+G51−@SUM(G53.G56)
59			
60	Interest expense	0	0
61	Other nonoperating expense	0	0
62	Other nonoperating income	0	0
63			
64	Profit before tax	+F58−F60−F61+F62	+G58−G60−G61+G62
65			

TABLE 8-1. (*Continued*)

A^a	B	C	D	E	F^b	G^c	H
66	Taxes				0	0	
67							
68	Profit after tax				+F64–F66	+G64–G66	
69					0	0	
70	Dividends						
71							

^{a}Labels begin in column A.
^{b}Year 1 data entered in column F.
^{c}Year 2 data entered in column G.

```
D 2 . D 2
C 3 . C 3
F 3 . G 3
F 6 . G 1 1
F 1 5 . G 1 8
F 2 3 . G 2 8
F 3 2 . G 3 9
F 4 4 . G 4 5
F 4 9 . G 4 9
F 5 3 . G 5 6
F 6 0 . G 6 2
F 6 6 . G 6 6
F 7 0 . G 7 0
```

After completing these entries, return the cursor to cell A1 by pressing the [Home] key. To save the worksheet template, invoke the {File Save} command, /FS. Lotus 1-2-3 will give the prompt, "Enter save file name." At that point, give the template a name of up to eight characters (alpha and numeric) such as cashflow.

Cash Flow Section: Direct Approach

Table 8-2 presents the cash flow statement using the direct approach. The cell references represent the mathematical formulas and logic statements responsible for the cash flow statement output. These entries refer to cell locations in the data input section in Table 8-1 and link the cash flow statement with the income statement and balance sheets.

The cash flow section of the template is not created as a separate worksheet but is added to the data input section created above in Table 8-1. If the data input section is not on the computer screen (in working memory of the computer, or RAM), it should be loaded before constructing the cash flow section of the template.

To load the data input file, place the data diskette in drive B and invoke the {File Retrieve} command, /FR. The program will give the prompt, "Enter name of file to retrieve" and will have the names of the files saved on the diskette highlighted on the screen. Using the arrow keys on the number pad on the right-hand side of the keyboard, move the cursor to the data input file (cashflow, in this example) and press the [Enter] key.

To begin the cash flow section of the template, move the cursor to the bottom of the template by pressing the [F5] or [GoTo] key. Respond to the computer prompt, "Enter address to go to," by typing A80 and pressing the [Enter] key. This will place the cursor at the bottom of the

TABLE 8-2. Cash Flow Statement: Direct Method

	A	B	C	D	E	F	G	H
80								
81		CASH FLOW: DIRECT FORMAT					+G3	
82								
83			Cash flows from operating activities					
84								
85			Net sales				+G44	
86				Plus (minus)				
87				Decrease (increase) in accounts receivable			+F8−G8	
88				Decrease (increase) in other current assets			+F11−G11	
89				Plus other operating income			+G45	
90								
91			Cash provided by operating activities				@SUM(G85.G89)	
92								
93								
94			Cost of sales				+G49	
95				Plus (minus)				
96				Increase (decrease) inventory			+G9−F9	
97				Decrease (increase) in payables			+F23−G23	
98				Decrease (increase) in other current liabilities			+F28−G28	
99								
100			Plus operating expenses (excluding depreciation)				+C53	
101				Plus (minus)				
102				Increase (decrease) in prepaids			+G10−F10	
103				Decrease (increase) in accruals			+F25−G25	

104	Plus other operating expenses	+G56
105	Plus interest expense	+G60
106		
107	Adjustments for income taxes	
108	Plus (minus)	
109	Income taxes (tax credits)	+G66
110	Decrease (increase) in taxes payable	+F26—G26
111	Decrease (increase) in deferred taxes	+F33—G33
112		
113	NET CASH FLOW FROM OPERATIONS	+G91—@SUM(G94,G96,G98,G100, G102,G105,G109,G111)
114		
115	Cash flows from investing activities	
116		
117	(Minus) other nonoperating expenses	—G61
118	Plus other nonoperating income	+G62
119	Plus (minus)	
120	Decrease (increase) in gross fixed assets	+F15—G15
121	Decrease (increase) in intangibles	+F17—G17
122	Decrease (increase) in other noncurrent assets	+F18—G18
123	Accumulated depreciation (sold)	—G55+(G16—F16)
124		
125	CASH USED (PROVIDED) IN INVESTING	@SUM(G117,G118,G120,G123)
126		

TABLE 8-2. Cash Flow Statement: Direct Method

	A	B	C	D	E	F	G	H
127		Cash flows from financing activities						
128								
129		Plus new borrowing						
130			Short-term notes payable				+G24	
131			Long-term debt			@IF(G27+G32−F32>0,G27+G32−F32,0)		
132			Less current debt amortization					
133			Short-term notes payable				−F24	
134			Current maturities long-term debt				−F27	
135			Additional LTD amortization			@IF(G27+G32−F32<0,G27+G32−F32,0)		
136			Plus (minus)					
137			Increase (decrease) other noncurrent liabilities				+G34−F34	
138			Increase (decrease) in preferred stock				+G35−F35	

139	Increase (decrease) in common stock	+G36−F36
140	Increase (decrease) in paid-in capital	+G37−F37
141	Retained earnings adjustment	+F39+G68−G70−G39
142	(Minus)	
143	Dividends paid	−G70
144	Increase in treasury stock	+F38−G38
145		
146	CASH PROVIDED (USED) IN FINANCING	+G130+G131+@SUM(G133.G135)+@SUM(G137.G141)+G143+G144
147		
148	CHANGE IN CASH AND EQUIVALENTS	+G113+G125+G146
149		
150		

data input section where the cash flow labels and formulas can be entered. The direct format cash flow statement is entered in cells A80 through H150, with labels in column A and formulas in column G. There will be no direct data input in this section of the template. Save the worksheet and complete the template by constructing the indirect cash flow format.

Cash Flow Section: Indirect Approach

Table 8-3 presents the cash flow statement using the indirect approach. To construct this section of the template, move the cursor to the right of the data input section by pressing the [F5] or [GoTo] key. Type I1 and press the [Enter] key in response to the "Enter address to go to" prompt. This will place the cursor to the right of the data input section; now enter the labels and formulas that make up the indirect cash flow format. This section of the template will be placed in cells I1 through P60, with labels in column I and formulas in column O. There is no data input in this section.

After all labels and formulas have been entered, save the entire template. Press the [Home] key and invoke the {File Save} command as discussed earlier.

The initial setup of the worksheet template will require a considerable amount of time, perhaps 1 to 2 hours depending on proficiency with the spreadsheet package. But after the template has been constructed and saved, it can be used repeatedly without difficulty. The process can even be customized by using macros, an advanced topic discussed later in this chapter.

DATA ENTRY AND RETRIEVAL

After the template has been constructed and saved as it appears in Tables 8-1 through 8-3, enter financial statement data, which are in the cells displayed with boldfaced type. The data include the identification information in cells A2 and D2 and the dollar denomination in cell C3. The template is set up to accept data for two consecutive years to be entered in columns F and G. Note that the total values on the data input sheet are not set up as data entries but are calculated by the worksheet formulas. This enables users to check totals from the original statements against the calculated totals to verify the accuracy of data input.

The spreadsheet will automatically recalculate all formulas in the worksheet after each data entry. But this slows down the process of entering data considerably. To speed up data entry, change to manual

TABLE 8-3. Cash Flow Statement: Indirect Method

	I	J	K	L	M	N	O	P
1								
2	CASH FLOW: INDIRECT FORMAT						+G3	
3								
4	Cash flows from operating activities							
5								
6	Net income						+G68	
7	Noncash items included in net income							
8	Plus depreciation and amortization						+G55	
9	Plus nonoperating expenses						+G61	
10	Minus nonoperating income						−G62	
11	Plus (minus)							
12	Decrease (increase) in accounts receivable						+F8−G8	
13	Decrease (increase) in inventories						+F9−G9	
14	Decrease (increase) in prepaids						+F10−G10	
15	Decrease (increase) in other current assets						+F11−G11	
16	Increase (decrease) in accounts payable						+G23−F23	
17	Increase (decrease) in other current liabilities						+G28−F28	
18	Increase (decrease) in accruals						+G25−F25	
19	Increase (decrease) in accrued taxes						+G26−F26	
20	Increase (decrease) in deferred taxes						+G33−F33	
21								
22	NET CASH FLOW FROM OPERATIONS						+O6+@SUM(O8.O1)+	
23							@SUM(O12.O20)	

TABLE 8-3. (*Continued*)

	I	J	K	L	M	N	O	P
24	Cash flows from investing activities							
25								
26	(Minus) other nonoperating expenses						−G61	
27	Plus other nonoperating income						+G62	
28	Plus (minus)							
29	Decrease (increase) in gross fixed assets						+F15−G15	
30	Decrease (increase) in intangibles						+F17−G17	
31	Decrease (increase) in other noncurrent assets						+F18−G18	
32	Accumulated depreciation (sold)						−G55+(G16−F16)	
33								
34	CASH USED (PROVIDED) IN INVESTING						@SUM(O26,O27,O29.O32)	
35								
36								
37	Cash flows from financing activities							
38								
39	Plus new borrowing							
40	Short-term notes payable						+G24	
41	Long-term debt						@IF(G27+G32−F32>0,G27+G32−F32,0)	
42	Less current debt amortization							
43	Short-term notes payable						−F24	
44	Current maturities long-term debt						−F27	
45	Additional LTD amortization						@IF(G27+G32−F32<0,G27+G32−F32,0)	

46	Plus (minus)	
47	Increase (decrease) other noncurrent liabilities	+G34–F34
48	Increase (decrease) in preferred stock	+G35–F35
49	Increase (decrease) in common stock	+G36–F36
50	Increase (decrease) in paid-in capital	+G37–F37
51	Retained earnings adjustment	+F39+G68–G70–G39
52	(Minus)	
53	Dividends paid	–G70
54	Change in treasury stock	+F38–G38
55		
56	CASH PROVIDED (USED) IN FINANCING	+40+O41+@SUM(O43.O45)+@SUM(O47.O51)+O53+O54
57		
58	CHANGE IN CASH AND EQUIVALENTS	+O22+O34+O56
59		
60		

recalculation. This is accomplished by invoking the {Worksheet Global Recalculate Manual} command, /WGRM and saving the template. Saved with this status designation, the worksheet formulas are recalculated only after pressing the [F9] or [Calc] key.

Once the data are entered into the income statement and balance sheet, the template automatically transfers the input according to the formulas and logic appearing in the cash flow section.

Printing the Entire Worksheet

To print the entire worksheet, return the cursor to cell A1 by pressing the [Home] key. The data input section containing the balance sheets and income statement can be printed by invoking the {Print Printer} command, /PP. At this point the user must specify various aspects of the print routine:

1. With the cursor highlighting "Range," press [Enter], type "A1.H70", and press [Enter].
2. With the cursor highlighting "Options," press [Enter], move the cursor to highlight "Setup," press [Enter], type "\015\027\047", and press [Enter]. Move the cursor to highlight "Page Length," press [Enter], type "88", and press [Enter]. This setup string is designed to print eight lines of condensed print per inch (instead of the usual six lines per inch on the Epson-type dot matrix printer). Different printers will require different setup strings. Consult the printer manual for variations on the setup string.
3. Type "QG" ("Quit" to return to the Print menu and "Go" to print the specified range). After the data input sheet is printed, type "P" to advance the paper to the top of the next page.

Note that the print options can be entered permanently in the template by following steps 1 and 2, then instead of step 3 typing "QQ", and finally saving the worksheet to invoke the print options automatically.

Printing Direct Cash Flow Format

The cash flow reports can be printed by following the same routine. To print the direct cash flow format, return the cursor to cell A80 by pressing the [GoTo] or [F5] key, type "A80", and then press [Enter]. The section is printed by invoking the {Print Printer} command, /PP. At this point the user must specify various aspects of the print routine:

1. With the cursor highlighting "Range," press [Enter], type "A80.H150", and press [Enter].

2. With the cursor highlighting "Options," press [Enter], move the cursor to highlight "Setup," press [Enter], type "\015\027\047", and press [Enter]. Move the cursor to highlight "Page Length," press [Enter], type "88", and press [Enter]. If this has been done in printing the data input section, step 2 may be skipped.

3. Type "QG" ("Quit" to return to the Print menu and "Go" to print the specified range). After the report is printed, type "P" to advance the paper to the top of the next page.

Printing the Indirect Cash Flow Format

The cursor must be moved to cell I1 to print the indirect cash flow format. The print routine is identical to that for the direct cash flow format, except the print range is specified as "I1.P60."

ACCRUAL AND CASH FLOW RATIOS

The cash flow section can be augmented by adding various accrual-based financial ratios or cash flow ratios. This will require adding a ratios section to the template in cells I60 through P140. It is beyond the scope of this chapter to provide a complete ratios template. But refer to Chapters 2 and 6 for the relevant accrual-based and cash flow ratios that might be included in such a template addition.

CUSTOMIZING TEMPLATES

An advanced technique to improve the efficiency of data entry and analysis is the *worksheet macro*. The technique requires writing a set of instructions for the computer to follow. The use of the macro to construct a worksheet menu will be illustrated.

The purpose of a worksheet menu is to combine several keystrokes into one to simplify various aspects of the analysis. Instead of going through the steps outlined above to print the various statements, for example, the routine can be programmed into a print menu with the use of several macros. Using the menu, printing can be accomplished through a single keystroke.

With the completed template loaded in the spreadsheet, the first step is to define and name all the possible ranges that are to be printed. This is accomplished by using the {Range Name Create} command, /RNC. In response to the following prompts, type

''Enter name:''	''Enter range:''
DATA	A1.H70
DIRECT	A80.H150
INDIRECT	I1.P60
MENU	Q2
\M	Q1

To construct the menu, move to an unused portion of the worksheet, press [F5] or [GoTo], and type "Q2". Beginning in cell Q2 and continuing to cell T2. Type the following labels in cells Q2, R2, S2, and T2, respectively:

```
DATA            DIRECT            INDIRECT            QUIT
```

Beneath each cell, type a brief description of the results of choosing that particular option. In cell Q3, for example, type "Prints data input file". This statement will appear in the second command line when the DATA selection is highlighted by the cursor.

In cell Q4, type the macro (command sequence) that is to be executed when the DATA selection is chosen. To print the data input sheet, the macro will read

```
' /PPRDATA~AGPQ
```

The command sequence reads {Print Printer Range DATA Enter Align Go Page Quit}, where DATA is the range A1.H70 and the tilde (˜) is equivalent to pressing the [Enter] key. Write a separate macro beneath each selection in row 4 to print each of the reports. To return to the READY mode, choose selection QUIT. The macro in cell T4, '/XQ˜, will instruct the computer to return to the READY mode. The Lotus 1-2-3™ command that automatically executes the menu should be typed as a macro in cell Q1. It reads, ' {Home} /XMMENU˜. When Alt-M is entered, the print menu will appear on the screen and look much like any other Lotus 1-2-3™ menu.

The cell entries for the print menu are as follows:

```
Q1    '{Home}/XMMENU~
Q2    'DATA
Q3    'Prints data input file
Q4    '/PPRDATA~AGPQ/XMMENU~
```

```
R2        'DIRECT
R3        'Prints cash flow direct
R4        '/PPRDIRECT~AGPQ/XMMENU~

S2        'INDIRECT
S3        'Prints cash flow indirect
S4        '/PPRINDIRECT~AGPQ/XMMENU~

T2        'QUIT
T3        'Returns to the READY mode
T4        '/XQ~
```

Menus can be set up to perform many different aspects of an analysis, including data entry, report viewing, and data saving and loading. The task, although straightforward, is not easy and should be attempted only after acquiring some familiarity with Lotus 1-2-3™.

SUMMARY

A worksheet template for generating cash flow statements identical to those discussed in Chapter 3 can be created using Lotus 1-2-3™ or similar spread sheet programs. In the template set up in this chapter, the simplified balance sheet and income statement in Table 8-1 served as the data input section. Tables 8-2 and 8-3 presented the cash flow statement using the direct and indirect formats, respectively.

Since the presentation of the cash flow statement is in a transitionary period, it is important that financial analysts have the ability to generate financial information in a standardized format. Templates will enable them to compare financial statements of firms in the same industry or for a single firm over time.

Glossary

Accounts receivable aging schedule. Traditional method of monitoring customer payment patterns. It involves creating a schedule showing end-of-month accounts receivable and percentages of outstanding receivables that are 1, 2, 3, and so on, months old.

Accrual-basis accounting. Method of accounting whereby revenues are recorded in the time period that coincides most closely to the completion of the transaction. The costs associated with each sale are recorded in the time period that best matches the sale. This is the preferred method of accounting for most business enterprises according to generally accepted accounting principles.

Cash-basis accounting. Method of accounting that records income when cash is actually received and expenses when payments are actually made. Individuals and some small businesses may use this technique to keep track of receipts and expenditures; however, it is inappropriate for most business operations.

Cash budget. A cash management tool that is used to forecast cash flow requirements. It is depicted by a schedule of cash receipts and cash disbursements over a specified time period.

Cash conversion period. A concept developed by Richards and Laughlin (1980) to measure the time interval between the delivery of inventory and the receipt of payment for items sold. It is calculated by subtracting days payable from the sum of days sales outstanding plus days inventory.

Cash flow cycle. Diagram depicting the manner in which assets are continuously changing form within the category of current assets.

Cash equivalents. Highly liquid securities with maturities of less than 90 days. They represent a low risk of loss in value due to changes in interest rates. This definition includes such instruments as money market funds, certificates of deposit, and treasury bills.

Cash flow from financing activities. Proceeds from new sources of financing such as new debt or equity less payments on loans and purchase of treasury stock. Dividend payments are also deducted.

Cash flow from investing activities. Nonoperating income and expenses along with purchases for new plant and equipment and receipts for asset liquidations.

Cash flow from operations. Difference between sales adjusted for the change in accounts receivable and operating expenses and cost of goods sold adjusted for accruals and payables. Interest expense is also deducted.

Current liquidity ratio. Ratio developed by Fraser (1983) to measure liquidity. It is calculated by combining cash assets (cash plus marketable securities) with cash flow from operations and dividing the result by current liabilities.

Defensive assets. Term used by Sorter and Benston (1960) to depict cash, marketable securities, and accounts receivable.

Direct format. Method of presenting the cash flow statement whereby cash inflows and cash outflows are computed directly. Prepared in this manner, a cash flow statement resembles a cash-basis income statement.

Financial flexibility. Term developed by Campbell, Johnson, and Savoie (1984) referring to the ability of a firm to take advantage of unexpected opportunities or respond to unexpected requirements by changing the amount and timing of cash flows. A firm's financial flexibility is determined by the stability of its earnings, affecting its ability to generate funds internally; the degree of leverage, affecting its access to external financing; and the availability of lines of credit.

Financing activities. Business transactions that relate to acquiring and servicing outside capital from both creditors and investors. These include borrowing money and repaying debts or otherwise retiring those loans.

Financing gap. This represents the lag between the time when payments for raw materials are made and receipts for finished products are received.

GAAP. Acronym for generally accepted accounting principles.

Indirect format. Method of preparing a cash flow statement that backs into cash flow from operations by removing the effects of accruals and deferrals that result in revenues and expenses but do not generate or use cash and by adjusting for operating receipts and expenditures of cash that do not result in revenues or expenses.

Interval analysis. Framework for studying liquidity developed by Sorter and Benston (1960). Several measures of liquidity are expressed as the number of days a firm can survive under specified conditions. Examples of intervals are the basic defensive interval, the no credit interval, the cash interval, and the reduced sales interval.

Investing activities. Business transaction involving the acquisition, disposition, and retirement of property, plant, and equipment or other productive assets. Transactions that involve the lending of money and collecting on those loans or the acquiring and disposing of equity instruments are also included.

Liquidity. Opportunity cost (including time and money) of converting assets into cash. The lower the cost, the more liquid the asset.

Liquidity Flow Index. Developed by Lemke (1970), it is the ratio of the practical maximum rate of cash outflow divided by the required rate of cash outflow.

Matching principle. Accrual accounting principle used to measure the profitability of sales by matching them with the appropriate expenses used to generate those sales. Only revenues and expenses that apply to current period transactions are included in the calculation of profit or loss.

Net liquid balance. Difference between the sum of cash, cash equivalents, and marketable securities and the sum of notes payable and current maturities of long-term debt.

Operating activities. All activities of an enterprise that are normally concerned with providing goods and services to customers and thus comprise the day-to-day operations of a business.

Operating revenues. Revenues that result from activities that are central to the ongoing operation. They may be sales, royalties, or rents.

Overtrading. A phenomenon that exists when a firm has an insufficient inventory to meet customer demand. The result is a high rate of inventory turnover and lost sales due to stockouts.

Payment pattern schedule. Method of tracking the collection of accounts receivable developed by Llewellen and Johnson (1972). It involves the linking of cash collections to the original sales that generated them. The basic approach is to determine the percentage of each month's sales that are collected in the month of the sale and the percentages collected in each of the subsequent months.

Productive assets.   Assets that are expected to generate revenues over a long period of time. They include property, plant, and equipment.

Quick assets.   Assets that are highly liquid, for example, cash, cash equivalents, and accounts receivable.

Realization principle.   Accrual accounting principle that records revenues in the time period that most closely coincides to the completion of the transaction that obligates the customer to pay.

Reconciliation method.   See indirect format.

Solvency.   In the event of a liquidation, when all the assets of a business are sold and the cash proceeds are sufficient to satisfy all financial obligations.

Spontaneous assets.   Assets that change proportionately with changes in sales. A spontaneous asset will increase by 10 percent when sales increase by 10 percent. This category of assets include cash, accounts receivable, inventory, and prepaids. Certain liabilities, including accounts payable and short-term accruals, are considered spontaneous liabilities.

Sustainable growth.   Concept developed by Higgins (1977) that approximates the level of sales growth that can be supported by the internally generated funds of an operation. Firms that grow faster than this rate must support their growth by changing investing or financing policies.

Working capital.   Accounting concept referring to a firm's investment in short-term assets; that is, cash, cash equivalents, accounts receivable, and inventory. *Net working capital* refers to the difference between current assets and current liabilities.

Working capital from operations.   A funds flow concept that is derived by adjusting net income for long-term accruals, deferrals, and other allocations that produce revenues and expenses but do not affect current accounts on the balance sheet.

Working capital pressure ratio.   Difference between the ratio of working capital requirements to sales and the profit margin on sales adjusted for dividend payout.

Working capital requirements.   Difference between the sum of accounts receivable and inventory and the sum of accounts payable and other accruals related to the firm's operations.

Worksheet macro.   A set of preprogrammed instructions for a spreadsheet program. Macros combine several keystrokes into one to simplify various aspects of spreadsheet analysis. The technique is often used to construct a worksheet menu.

Worksheet template.   A standardized worksheet with all relevant titles, formulas, and logic statements for a specific application.

Index

185